CONTENTS

Title Page	3
Dedication	5
Chapter 1: So you need to learn about user experience	7
Chapter 2: The Common Sense Guide to UX	13
Chapter 3: What is UX and why should I care?	19
Chapter 4: Who does what now?	24
Chapter 5: Opening the Black Box	32
Chapter 6: Your UX Department	67
Chapter 7: Interview Guide	78
Chapter 8: Conclusion	89
References	91
About The Author	93

THE MANAGER'S UX SURVIVAL GUIDE

Kraig Finstad

To Erica, Brielle, and Ronan

CHAPTER 1: SO YOU NEED TO LEARN ABOUT USER EXPERIENCE

Congratulations, you've been put in charge of your department's user experience group!

No?

Condolences...you've been asked to *build* a user experience capability from scratch and don't know where to start.

Maybe some other situation? No matter - the problem is you need to learn about user experience, or UX, and don't know much about it. There are two ways we can do this. If you need results, fast, and/or need to put on a good show for upper management, go to Chapter Two. There you'll learn how to weasel your way through it. You'll receive valuable tips for building a Potemkin village of UXers, happily doing whatever it is UXers do. You won't know precisely what they're doing, but neither will upper management. Soon you'll be able to show management things like prototypes and surveys and usability test reports. Or at least you'll be able to show management some stuff that's *called* those things.

But that path isn't for everyone. If you know anything at all about the discipline of UX and how it's practiced, or if you genu-

inely care about your end users, or your company's bottom line, you'll skip to Chapter Three. There you'll learn some of the basics, such as how UX came to be and what kinds of methodologies you will become familiar with in later chapters. There will also be some background on UX practitioners. Understanding the nuts and bolts of UX matters because what you're going to get out of a UX team is going to be different from what you're probably used to. With many disciplines in systems development the deliverables are concrete:
- Business analysts deliver requirements documents
- Developers deliver working software systems
- Trainers deliver classes and online courses
- Database admins deliver databases
- ...And so on

UX design delivers concrete things like prototypes and screens with icons, but with a lot of hidden knowledge supporting those design decisions. Often what UX Research is going to deliver is *insight*. This usually takes the form of reports and/or presentations.

Later, after you've got some real UX knowledge under your belt, you can go back and take a look at Chapter Two for laughs.

Further on you'll learn about things like UX maturity models, establishing a true UX competency, and becoming an advocate for UX through more comprehensive presentations to larger organizations.

Toward the end there's a template of interview questions you can use to make sure the UX people you're hiring know their stuff, even if it's new to you.

This book isn't intended to be a cookbook to show you how to get a usability test up and running. It is also not going to show you how to implement UX in an Agile vs Waterfall environment. Those are things that should be up to your UX experts. What it will do is help you understand enough about the field to get the right people in place to make UX work for your company.

What exactly are we talking about?

It happens every time. I have my phone in position above my dashboard, the car is running, and I'm ready to go. I start my GPS map app so I can get to my destination, it starts to slowly load... and an ad appears, demanding my attention. I click the little "x" to close it...and it takes me to a download page, ignoring my request to dismiss. I switch back to the map and it's having trouble figuring out where I am. To make matters worse, some controls look like buttons, some look like icons, and some look like plain text but can be tapped. Once I get my destination finally entered, I touch the Start button but nothing happens, over and over. The app is slow to respond to taps and has no feedback mechanism, so the wrong thing gets pressed when the app finally refreshes. *Finally* the map itself appears, but in landscape orientation there's a big info bar at the top (with a lot of empty space), and it's mirrored by a big info bar at the bottom (with a lot of empty space). The map is squeezed into a much smaller-than-it-should-be window in the middle. It feels like a 1990s web browser suffering from an acute toolbar infection. But this is a modern UI on modern hardware! Why is interacting with computers still so problematic? This short example highlights usability issues, human factors safety issues, and performance and responsiveness issues. It all adds up to a poor user experience. Does this sound like the kind of experience you'd want associated with your company?

Imagine this situation

It's another drawn-out project meeting, and someone from Marketing is delivering the bad news about how your new product's UI redesign is not going over well with users. Sales are lower, online ratings are lower, but complaints are sure up. What went wrong?

• Developers took the old version's UI and brought it up to date using the latest "industry standard" icon and control libraries.

• Quality Assurance did User Acceptance Testing to make sure users could get through a script, providing evidence that the

business requirements were being fulfilled.
• Systems Analysts did A/B testing with a beta version vs. the old version. The results showed that the new version took fewer clicks than the old version to complete a task.
• Marketing solicited prerelease feedback through an email campaign. The people who responded said the new version was fine.

So what happened? Well, none of these different efforts were really designed to understand your users. There was no direct observation of users in the field. The UI design was mostly determined by a different company and just "plugged in." There was no controlled experiment comparing user performance on the beta version vs. the old version, focused on data like task failures and error rates. There was a lot of selection bias in the feedback gathered, providing an unrealistic picture of user attitudes. This outcome could have been avoided with a proper effort aimed at improving the user experience, with UX designers and UX researchers combining efforts to provide guidance on building a system that works the way the users need.

Now imagine this situation.

You've recently hired a database administrator for a project, and you specifically needed someone who was an expert in SQL and Access. Let's call him Database Dave. Database Dave has been working away in his cubicle the past few weeks putting together the SQL database you hired him for. The going is slow, and his weekly status reports don't really indicate much beyond that progress is being made behind the scenes. In a recent project review meeting he presented some of his ideas on data structures by drawing rows and columns on a whiteboard, but without showing any screenshots. At the end of the meeting you ask him to do a demo of the database for the project team in one week's time, regardless of how incomplete it is. He says "No problem!" and goes back to his work. A week later in the next project team meeting he hooks his laptop up to a projector and fires up Access. He walks the project team through a few SQL queries. It's more rudimentary than you'd hoped, but it was a relief to see more than sketches on a whiteboard. After the meeting, however, the slacker version of Database Dave re-emerges and again progress is slow. A couple more weeks go by and the project is officially delayed. Database Dave has a working version of the database that is almost done, and every time you ask him why it's taking so long he says things like "that's just the way it is" and "these things take time." You decide to ask your team lead about the situation to see if she has any insights. She admits that a lot of the delay is due to Dave not really knowing what he's doing. He is constantly asking her how to do things, and appeared to not really know the difference between a database and a spreadsheet. Turns out Database Dave is really more of an Excel Elmo, more familiar with formulae and cells than fields and queries. Since databases share a lot in common with spreadsheets, at least superficially, he thought he could fake it until he makes it and learn along the way. Unfortunately for "Dave", it's hard to become an expert by relying on YouTube videos and your coworkers.

Is the above likely to happen in real life? Probably not. I'm using an established discipline in systems development to illustrate a real problem in another one, that being user experience. UX is not as established yet. As such, as a hiring manager or project manager, you could find yourself stuck with the UX equivalent of a Database Dave. It may be because you don't have any UX people on board yet to help vet candidates, or it could be that you're now in charge of a team or project where people without the right skills are already in place.

How this book will help

A major point of this book is to help you understand user experience, not so you can do it yourself, but so you can identify the right people for the right job and tell the difference between great deliverables and poor ones. Just like you wouldn't want Database Dave on your team, you don't want UX people who can't really do what's in their job descriptions. A database resembles a spreadsheet but isn't one, and a usability test resembles a user acceptance test but isn't one. With the information in this book you will

be able to:
• Evaluate the skill sets of your UX team members.
• Get the right balance of specializations. You don't want a UX team of people who are good at interviewing users but nothing else.
• Understand what makes for a useful and valuable UX report or design.
• Interview job candidates with more confidence about UX skills.
• Start building towards a more mature UX capability that will make a real difference to your company.

This book is a bit of a departure for me as up until now my non-fiction writing has been for journals in the fields of Psychology and Human-Computer Interaction. That type of writing is full of methodology notes, statistics, and literature reviews with lots and lots of citations. I'm purposely avoiding that level of detail here. What I want to do is get you the information you need about UX quickly and effectively, and to do that I've included lots of real-world stories but not a lot of reliance upon studies. I wanted to have some fun writing this, and for you to have some fun reading it.

CHAPTER 2: THE COMMON SENSE GUIDE TO UX

Caution!

In engineering circles, there's an old saying that a project's options are: (1) Cheap, (2) Fast, and (3) Good. But you can only choose two. For example, if you choose Fast and Good, it won't be Cheap. In this section we're going to pretend like we can violate this guideline and get everything done right, and fast, with almost no extra money! It's the Common Sense Guide to UX, your shortcut to UX success! It should be obvious by now that this is not meant to be taken seriously.

User experience is just common sense

There's really nothing to it. You don't need to be a psychologist to understand what people need in an interface. You just ask them! Maybe if you want to be really technical you hold a focus group and ask them all at once. Write down what they say and take it to development. Throw that list over the wall, as it were. Sit back and watch the features get added while user satisfaction goes up. And how will you measure user satisfaction? Well, ask the users again. It's just common sense. And don't worry about those annoying details like what colors work best, or font sizes, or screen layouts. There are corporate standards for that.

Here are some examples of how UX is just common sense:
- They say there's safety in numbers, and this is true for ideas

as well. Brainstorming in a big group is a great way to come up with the best product features without needing to do long-term research.

• It's OK to have a busy interface with a lot going on, like mixing audio and video and text. The modern office environment has trained people to be good multitaskers.

• If users have trouble using your website, they'll tell you. Slap on a feedback button and anyone with a gripe will let you know.

• If problems persist, you can fix it with training. Any system deficiency can be overcome with training, quick start guides, job aides, and technical documents. Pile 'em on. Your users may be slow using the system, and they may not like it, but it's supposed to be work, not fun. If it's their job, they have to do it if they want to keep receiving a paycheck.

Anyone can do UX

Since UX is just common sense, it follows that anyone (well, anyone with common sense) can do UX. Why pay through the nose for some egghead PhD who specializes in Human-Computer Interaction when you can just have someone from Marketing do that focus group you've got in mind? It doesn't take special skills to ask people what they want, or write it down, or hand the results to the developers. Nowadays UX specialists come from all kinds of fields. There are the classics like psychology and anthropology, but you'll also find UX people with backgrounds in photography, marketing, fine arts, and business administration. What matters is the job title. If someone has the title "user experience researcher," that means they can do user experience research. Besides, what matters in UX is *passion*. If you have a passion for user experience, you can do anything. If you really, really care about the end users, you'll do what's right. It will all come together.

Science doesn't matter, what matters is feelings

We all want to feel good about our jobs, our products, our careers. We want our users to feel good about the systems we design. That's why the primary metric we should be concerned with is "user delight." If we're not delighting our users, we've failed. If they're not delighted, they won't recommend our product to their friends and families. That's why you don't need to hire researchers who know how to measure things like quantified usability using 7-point Likert scales, or who can tell you if an interface with 3 task failures is really better than an interface with 4 task failures. No, you just need to ask your users if they're delighted or not. If you want to get really fancy, you can ask for smiley face ratings. For example, just look at these two example survey items:

1. This system meets my requirements.

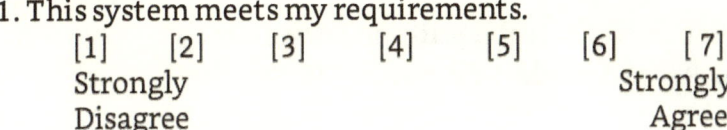

2. How do you like this system?

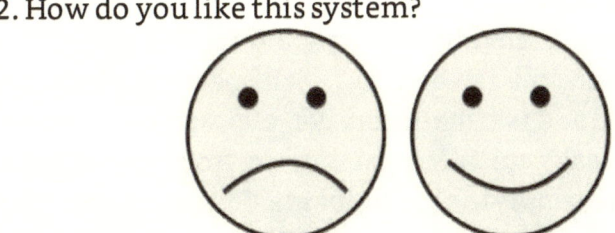

The first one is cold and boring. People are less likely to feel engaged with a survey like that. The second one is fun and inviting! If you want to get all scientific about it, you can calculate percentages of smiles vs. frowns. Maybe even have someone who is really good at Excel adjust the size of the faces to represent user delight based on the data, like this:

Kraig Finstad

Now you have a visual indicator that the smiley face is bigger than the sad face, which is a great indicator of user delight!

Don't sweat the technical details and documents

You've heard people talk about things like "Usability Test Reports." That sounds impressive, and you're sure upper management would be impressed if your department started producing things titled "Usability Test Report." The trouble is, usability testing is *expensive*. It involves having a qualified practitioner observe users, often in a lab setting, with specialized software. Recruiting users alone is time-intensive, and you might have to burn some political capital to get buy-in from other departments who will be supplying participants. There are such things called "Discount Usability Testing" and "Guerrilla Usability Testing" - those are techniques aimed to get a lot done with few participants and focus on problem solving rather than quantitative conclusions. What you could try is "Deep Discount Usability Testing": pull some people from the hallway into a conference room, maybe one with a quick "Usability Lab" sign posted out front. Ask them about the features in your product, ask them how they would approach tasks, and write up the results. Don't worry about things like error rates, time on task, creating a highlight video, eye tracking, or any of that. Summarize it in PowerPoint, call it "Usability Test Report", and you're set.

Another technique you may have heard of is heuristic evaluation. It sounds good in theory - you have one or more UX experts go through an interface and compare its features to these known principles of human-computer interaction called heuristics. Having one person evaluate your interface sounds great, as it's a lot less expensive than having a bunch of people come in for a usability test. The problem is those pesky heuristics that require some education and experience to apply correctly. But heuristics are really just rules of thumb, so what you could do is just have someone do the evaluation and ignore the heuristics. Have them go through the system and jot down any notes about things that feel "off" to them. Look at the notes and put together a nice Executive Summary - that's what upper management is going to pay attention to anyway.

When it comes to building user interfaces, just trust your developers. You can ask if they're using the latest libraries from corporations like Google - that way the UX Research is baked in and you can just apply it. This way there's no need to build early screen prototypes, or document the user interface.

All you need is work

Make sure your UX team is producing test reports, evaluations, site maps, or whatever. That's what's important. You don't need anything like a vision, or a comprehensive UX maturity model on which to focus your sights. Once what you're doing starts producing results, other departments are sure to notice and start doing similar things in their own projects. Eventually your company will have a solid UX culture and be producing world-class, user-delighting products.

Developers do the hard stuff, UX makes it pretty

From the This Really Happened Files:

I was in a training about Requirements Gathering, and we had just completed the introductions where everyone in the class announced their name and job role. At the time my title was "Human Factors Engineer" and I was responsible primarily for usability testing, user research, prototyping, and screen design. The

instructor voiced some recognition for the role, saying she had a background in user-centered design herself. Later she was talking about the different roles in projects and summarized a part of the development process as "The software developers build it and then you guys" (pointing at me) "...make it all pretty."
/End of File

So there you have it. The job of human factors engineers, UX researchers, usability engineers, UX designers - their job is to take what software developers do and make it pretty. And, since this is the superficial stuff that's done last, it's OK to bring in your UX resources at the very end of the project after all the hard work of building the system is already done.

CHAPTER 3: WHAT IS UX AND WHY SHOULD I CARE?

What UX is and is not (for real this time)

For those of you joining from Chapter 1, this is where things really start. Those who started in Chapter 2 are either here, reading on to see how to do UX correctly, or they're off making the world a worse place by perpetuating all that wrongheadedness. I know I started off this book with a lot of myths to be debunked, but this part is more serious. The majority of this book is about what UX is and how it works, but I want to take some time to talk about what UX is not.

UX is not rocket science. If fact, anymore, it's not much of *any* science. As more and more people became attracted to the field, it suffered a sort of regression to the mean in terms of the scientific ability of its practitioners. This was waved away with dismissive proclamations of UX being more "art than science," of the need to "empathize" with users (rather than observe and understand them), and how having a "passion" for UX is what you need to do the job. I've had some managers placed in charge of my departments because they were passionate (and ignorant) about UX. By this token it logically follows that the manager should have been able to pitch in and do UX work too, being equally qualified and all. Just get in there and start empathizing.

It shouldn't be this way. Your UX team should be smarter

than you about design, analysis, and human psychology, and you should be OK with that. You don't want "feel good" UXers who will bless designs and tell you everything is fine with your software. You want just the opposite. You want methodical specialists who will mercilessly tear down your systems so that they can be rebuilt. The rest of this book is designed to help you identify those people and understand their contributions.

Getting to know user experience

Now for some real background. As a field, user experience evolved from usability engineering, or sometimes just "usability." It may help to think of the usability of a system in terms of how easy it is to learn, use, and remember. There are other factors, and other definitions, but this one works for now. The discipline of usability engineering therefore is helping build systems with the user in mind, to make them usable. This involves studying people in their workplaces as they use the systems you're interested in improving (like Version 1 to Version 2) or replacing (like physical phones with a computerized system). It also involves building prototypes to test out, conducting tests, analyzing data, reporting results, and influencing stakeholders to make changes that take user needs into account. User experience expands upon this by making it more about people than about the systems they use. The International Organization for Standardization (ISO) defines of user experience in ISO-9241 as "a person's perceptions and responses that result from the use or anticipated use of a product, system or service" (ISO, 1998).

What others may think about UX

You need to understand how others in your org may respond to the idea of incorporating user experience practices. If everyone is on board, great! If not, be prepared for people arguing against investing in UX. Pushback may come in a simple form, such as "Our product is selling fine, we must be doing something right." Developers may see screen design as the fun part of their job and resent that task being assigned to someone else. Understanding users in a simple way may be part of requirements gathering, usually the purview of business analysts. System usage from the user perspective may be overseen by Quality Assurance with its User Acceptance Testing. This book will help you address these and other concerns as you work to develop user experience in your company.

Here's why you (and everyone in your org) should care about UX.

Time is money. In product development, the more time you save, the more money you save. Spending unnecessary time means spending unnecessary money. You may be tempted to just have the market work it out. Let the Invisible Hand work its magic. The trouble is, that hand is *slow*. If you rely on customer feedback, acceptance, rejection, delight, disgust, etc., think of all the time and money you spent on product development and marketing, only to release something that nobody wants to buy or recommend to others. If you catch what's stinking up your product early on, say during the prototype phase, you can fix it *before* you pay for developers to develop and marketers to market. You'll have a product that's been through the wringer: subjected to real usage scenarios, real users, and analyzed by experts trained in human-computer interaction. *That's* the real bottom line argument for user experience research and design. *That's* why you should care. It's great to have a passion for design, or an interest in research, or to care about your users. But that's not good enough for upper management. They're in it for the money, and they need to know how UX is going to help the company make more.

From the This Really Happened Files:

Enterprise software is a tough beast to tame. Projects have multiple developers, business analysts, systems analysts, UX practitioners, trainers, and thousands of users waiting to use and abuse (and be abused by) the new system. One such project was an internal purchasing system that let our company's employees go through our supply network and fill up a virtual shopping cart. Any such system is going to need a solid information architecture to allow easy browsing of categories, and a search engine that helps users find what they need. According to the QA testers, the critical search function was performing well; i.e, it wasn't generating any bug reports in user acceptance testing where the users were given scripts like "Search for pencils." The system would find "pencils" and populate a screen of suppliers and prices. No problem there! Downstream development fixes averted! However, I took the system into usability testing and found a big concern. Users weren't always able to find laptop computers in the new system. It would work if they knew exactly what brand name they wanted, and it would work if they searched for "notebook," but it would return zero results if the user searched for "laptop." All the portable computers in the database were called "notebooks" and the system wasn't smart enough to know that in the user's mind "laptop" was an equivalent term. I called this the "laptop/notebook problem" in presentations to management and it was a powerful argument for fixing the system. I did a follow up study to determine what kinds of terms people used in their searches, which were compiled as we looked to improve the system. We only had the resources to implement a brute-force approach by attaching aliases that pointed to the correct database entry, like this:

- "Laptop" -> Notebook
- "PC" -> Personal Computer
- "Desktop" -> Personal Computer
- "Hardware" -> H/W (yes, it was really in the database description like this due to character limits)
- "Software" -> S/W (ditto)
- ...And so on

Remember, this wasn't a bug in the traditional sense, but finding the issue and resolving it early saved the company not only the multiple thousands of dollars it would have cost to fix the system after it had been deployed, it saved additional money by warding off tech support calls from incredulous users who couldn't believe their new purchasing system didn't know what a laptop was.

/**End of File**

Beginner's Mind

One of my favorite Zen stories is about a master carver named Kosen, whose carving over the gate at a temple in Kyoto says "The First Principle." It is regarded as a masterpiece of the art of calligraphy. In preparing a carving, Kosen would sketch the design on paper first, and this required ink. One of his students, who tended to be outspoken and critical of his master, would assist the process by preparing the ink. When Kosen first sketched out "The First Principle," this student was not impressed and said, "That is not so good." Another attempt failed as well - "Poor - worse than the first one." On and on it went, until Kosen had made 84 sketches. At last the student had to step away for a bit, and Kosen saw his chance to work without the student's scrutiny. He hurriedly sketched "The First Principle" with a mind clear of distraction. "A masterpiece," declared the student.

I think this story applies to the UX world because it turns the traditional idea of teacher and student on its head, and the teacher really learns something. If you are new to the world of UX, it may seem natural to have your experienced UX practitioners teach you what they know about their world. Similarly, they probably have much to learn from you. When approaching a new project it is often useful to adopt the Zen concept of *shosin*, or "Beginner's Mind." Adopting the mindset of a naive user helps us understand how intimidating a new system can be, or how cumbersome an old legacy system can be, in order to start the process of improvement. Don't expect a UXer to jump into a project and begin immediately solving problems - this early adjustment of perspective is a bit time consuming but critical to the process. Be patient. However, when it comes to things like building a presentation for maximum effect with stakeholders, many UXers really are beginners and will look to you for guidance. Student and teacher roles become two-way streets.

CHAPTER 4: WHO DOES WHAT NOW?

Practitioners

User experience is said to be a multi-disciplinary pursuit. This means that you get your best results when people with a variety of backgrounds are involved in your product's research and design. That said, you want to make sure your UXers are able to really do their job. User experience design is *not* the same thing as graphic design, and user experience research is *not* the same thing as market research.

From the This Really Happened Files:

I was involved in interviewing a candidate for the position of user experience researcher. Since she was coming from a marketing background, I wanted to get a sense of her abilities with scientific research. I asked if she had experience with quantitative as well as qualitative studies and to describe them. She confidently replied that yes, she had experience with both "qual" and "quant" studies. I asked her to elaborate, specifically on what qualified as "quant." She said that qualitative studies were just like regular surveys, but quantitative studies were those where you surveyed enough people to get statistical significance. Well, this is just flat out wrong on several levels. First, there is an, ahem, qualitative difference between qualitative and quantitative studies. Qualitative studies gather qualitative data, things like words, impressions, likes, dislikes. Quantitative studies gather quantitative data, things like numbers, ratings on a scale, amount of errors. It's not just a matter of scaling. Racking up the number of

participants on a qualitative survey does not suddenly make it a quantitative survey; it makes it a large-scale qualitative survey. Second, "quantitative" does not mean statistically significant. We'll get into significance elsewhere, but real quick that means your finding is probably not a fluke. Plenty of quantitative studies do not achieve statistical significance, and there are times when the absence of significance is important and worth reporting. Other studies are just not designed with the statistical power to achieve significance because that's not the point of the study. Statistical significance is associated with higher sample sizes, but it isn't a causal relationship.
/End of File

Lesson learned: People coming into UX from a different field may speak a different technical language, one that may be incompatible with doing UX correctly. Don't hire a marketing or business person to do statistical analysis if they're speaking their native tongue. The difference between qualitative and quantitative studies is so important that's one of the first interview questions you'll find at the end of the book.

The field of user experience has evolved in recent years away from generalists and towards specialists. Human Factors Engineering is still a discipline, but is no longer so closely associated with software experience design. Years ago, software Human Factors Engineers were responsible for:
- User interviews and observations
- User interface design
- Prototyping
- Usability testing
- Statistical analysis and reporting

In other words, they were generalists. Their backgrounds were often things like:
- Human-Computer Interaction

- Cognitive Psychology
- Engineering Psychology
- Computer Science

As software human factors engineering and then usability engineering evolved into user experience, it became more and more rare to have one individual responsible for all these duties. Nowadays, anthropologists are often hired for field interviews and "ethnography." The quotes are there because real ethnography is almost never practiced - these researchers are observing business tasks over a few hours or workdays, not entire lives for months or years. Graphic artists develop low-fidelity, non-interactive prototypes, and front-end developers build high-fidelity, interactive prototypes. Usability testing is actually a range of techniques and is conducted by experimental/cognitive psychologists, human-computer interaction specialists, or others depending on complexity. Statistics are often just ignored by an organization because math is hard or something. In a typical organization it's common to see "user experience researchers" and "user experience designers." Someone working at a more strategic level may have the title "User Experience Architect." Some organizations have "User Experience Directors" or even "Vice President of User Experience." A UX designer is likely building site maps and screens. A UX researcher is taking those screens and testing how users react to them. A UX Architect is guiding the end-to-end experience of the user. A UX Director is responsible for the experience of several products or a product line. A UX VP is doing something...somewhere...maybe evangelizing UX throughout the company? I'm not sure because I've never seen one but I've heard they exist.

UX Researchers

The job of a UX researcher is to understand your users and explain them to you, your project teams, management, etc. in ways that are actionable. They employ a variety of techniques to do so, as will be explained later. They also help UX designers put together new or improved interfaces that will address the usability issues they find in their studies. Being able to do all this requires experience and training in the scientific method, knowledge of data gathering techniques, and analysis and presentation skills.

From the This Really Happened Files:

One of my recently-hired researcher colleagues asked me what the best way was to show how many times each issue was mentioned in a survey. He warned me up-front that he didn't have any experience in statistical software. I looked at his list of issues and said he could just use Excel to build a pivot table for an easy frequency distribution. Or, maybe not so easy. It turns out not only did he not know how to build a pivot table, he didn't know what a frequency distribution was. His background was in visual arts and he was a "self taught" researcher with no formal training.
/End of File

Background is important. In other software development disciplines you can't get away with this kind of lack of experience. If you're hired as a Java developer, you need to be able to sit down and start coding in Java on Day One, not pick it up as you go because the only language you ever learned was Visual Basic. Having a "passion" for user experience is no substitute for training or real world experience, especially if it means you need to lean on others to do your work for you. When you hire a UX researcher, you need to be sure he or she can do the job. As you're this far into the book, you know that UX is not just common sense. Down the line you'll learn more about what methods and deliverables you can expect from a UX researcher. At the end of the book you'll be equipped with interview questions that will help you pinpoint just how prepared a job candidate is to hit the ground running and start delivering research insights instead of asking other people how to do things beyond talking to users (and even that requires training and experience to do right).

When doing your due diligence on the background of researchers, ask about degrees in addition to titles. I've seen UX researchers refer to themselves as "psychologists" when their highest degree is a Masters. Applied psychologists have PhDs in things like cognitive and engineering psychology. A Masters in Human-Computer Interaction is often a good fit for a UX researcher position, but there will be less emphasis there on quantitative analysis. Not every UX researcher you hire needs to be a bona fide statistician. However, they should all (and I mean *all*) be able to do the basics of data analysis. This means understanding how to collect unbiased data, the fundamentals of data visualization, and basic statistics (measures of central tendency like mean/median/mode, standard deviation, counts vs. percentages, and frequency distributions). You don't need a department of people doing Analysis of Variance (ANOVA) and multiple regressions, but having someone onboard who can do those things and double-check the work of others is very valuable. Just be sure that they can really do those things, not just run the software to generate numbers.

From the This Really Happened Files:

At one of my jobs I was the double-checker for statistics work. One of the other researchers wanted me to verify that her ANOVA on survey data about an application was correct and the significant finding she had found was valid. She was concerned that her small sample size (N = 8) meant that she wouldn't be able to generalize her findings. It was a good question, because it's very common for ANOVA to work best with larger samples. I started by asking how representative her sample really was - was this a tiny portion of the user base or not? She said, "No, that's all of them." It turns out this was a very specialized application only used by a total of eight people. I told her that running an ANOVA didn't make any sense in this case. ANOVA is an inferential statistics technique; you infer from a sample and generalize to a population. If you gather data from an entire population (in this case eight people), you don't need to infer anything with statistics - any differences you find are really there. This was an example of someone running stats software and looking for important findings without understanding the fundamentals of the underlying scientific principles. When you hire a researcher to answer questions with data, make sure they know statistics and not just statistics software. Statistics programs do what you tell them to do, but knowing what to tell them to do is not trivial. Serious training in statistics is required to know which method to use and how to interpret the output.

/End of File

When hiring a UX researcher, you need to think long-term. You may have a pressing need to get a survey done for a big project, but if you hire someone who only has experience with surveys you're going to get what you pay for. After the survey project is done and a different style of research is warranted, you need your researcher to adapt and figure out the best methodology. This is where scientific training is so crucial - figuring out what the real research question is, *before* going off and collecting data, is the key to a successful project.

UX Designers

The job of a UX designer is to build user interfaces that people can actually use effectively. It's not just graphic design - a UX designer needs to understand the human-computer interaction principles of design as well as the aesthetic ones. Have you ever visited a website that seemed to be just a photograph? Maybe it was a beautiful outdoor scene, maybe it was something abstract. You probably thought, first, "This is different!" Then, after looking at the picture for a bit with nothing happening on-screen, you probably thought, "Is it broken? What do I do now?" This may have led to some experimentation, like scooting the mouse cursor around for hot spots, maybe give the old scroll wheel a spin. Eureka! Scrolling moved some text up and over the picture from down below the fold. Now you can see the real website. It was just hidden from view for the sake of a splashy intro, with no visual indicator of how you interact with the site to get the information you need. This is pure graphic design, not UX design.

A job interview for a UX designer position should be much more visual than one for a UX researcher. They should arrive with a portfolio of the work they've done, and you may need to arrange ahead of time to be in a room with good projection capabilities because the portfolio will often be digital. Clarify up front with your company's security if it's possible to have a personal laptop brought in, and inform the candidate appropriately. If not, be sure you have a system they can use with a flash drive, or if that's prohibited too, a Dropbox or similar account.

From the This Really Happened Files:
I was helping interview a candidate for a UX designer position and the candidate had experience primarily in UX Research. He liked the Design aspect more and wanted to move in that direction. His portfolio mostly consisted of things like banners for websites. They were competently done, although nothing special. But what really stood out was that he had nothing to demonstrate that was an end-to-end interaction. No full screen designs, no icons, no buttons. It wasn't a good fit for us because we needed someone who could design interactions, not just web page elements.
/End of File

A UX designer needs to be able to demonstrate designing screens, preferably by incorporating the findings from a research effort. Designers should have experience with software like Illustrator and Photoshop, as well as prototyping tools like Azure and Balsamic. When you're trying to fill a UX Design position, make sure the candidates can really produce prototypes that UX Research can take into usability testing. Making beautiful static images isn't enough; the screens need to be interactive. True development skills may be too much, though - the ability to write code may be useful if you don't have dedicated front-end developers, but it's more important for UX designers to be well-versed in usability principles than software development. UX Designers need to be able to speak the same language as UX researchers when they collaborate on designs. After a research study is complete, the researcher should be working with the designer to help inform the next iteration of the software so that it solves the issues that were found.

CHAPTER 5: OPENING THE BLACK BOX

Introduction to Methods

I've often likened my role as a UX practitioner to being a 'black box.' Things like requirements and issues go in one side as input, and on the other side there are things like reports and designs as output. It's like a black box because my management never really understood what happened between the input and output.

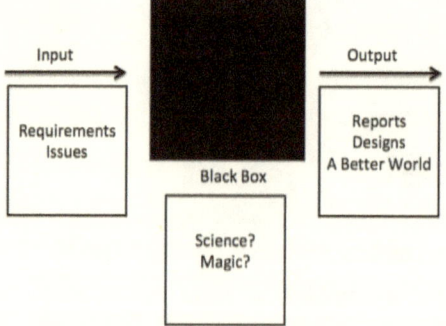

In this section I'd like to open the box, peek inside, and show you what UXers are actually doing. User experience practitioners engage in a wide variety of activities. At least, they should. First, here's a bunch of stuff that can go wrong.

Imagine your department's VP asked if one of your UX people could help out another org and do some User Acceptance Testing. You could politely inform him that just because UAT has "User" in it doesn't mean it's within the scope of UX responsibility. UAT is accomplished with scripts and basically just lets you know if the system works, if it's buggy, or if it doesn't satisfy a business requirement. Nothing burns out UX practitioners faster than being shunted into areas that they can maybe do, but for which they're not specialized (or for which they didn't put in years of school).

Similarly, if you have a UX researcher who:
- Conducts lots and lots of user interviews
- Generates reports that highlight issues but not solutions
- Says usability testing is a waste of time
- Doesn't contribute to the design process

...you've probably got someone who *should* be taken out of UX and put into User Acceptance Testing. These are the hallmarks of someone with a very limited toolbox. A real UX researcher should be doing things like:
- Usability Testing
- Task Analysis
- Heuristic evaluation
- Surveys
- Data analysis
- Reporting issues and suggesting solutions

A real UX designer should be doing things like
- User flows
- Site maps
- Screen/icon/button design
- UI look and feel guidelines
- Building prototypes

Understanding what your UXers are doing will help you be a better UX advocate and manager in general. What follows in this section is not an exhaustive list of UX methods, but it covers the activities your UX department will be conducting most often.

Research: Usability Testing

Usability testing is one of your UX researcher's primary responsibilities. A usability test is an evaluation of a system (like a computer application) performed in a controlled environment. How controlled is a matter of debate. Very formal usability tests often take place in labs resembling psychology labs, with one-way mirrors and recording equipment. Informal tests can be done in a conference room with nothing more than notes being taken for later analysis. What's common across all usability tests is that they are both structured and open-ended. While planning for the test, the UX researcher will coordinate with business analysts (or another subject matter expert) and put together a usability test script. The script is a set of tasks that the usability test participants will read and attempt to carry out in the system. The script is the structure; the open-ended component is that the participant is to complete the task any way they can. A usability test script item might read "Using this system, find the best deal on a sectional sofa." It should *not* be something like "Use the search function to find a sectional sofa. Be sure to use the word 'couch,' though, because the system doesn't know the word 'sofa.' Use the sort function on the results to find the lowest price." You *want* to find problems in the system so you can solve them, and that's why your UX researcher shouldn't give participants a garden path to walk down to make development and management feel like they made a great system on the first try.

Usability tests often rely on prototypes, or preliminary models, for new systems. Prototypes will be developed by a UX designer, possibly with the assistance of a front end developer. The level of complexity of a prototype is referred to as its *fidelity*. A low-fidelity prototype might be sketches on pieces of paper, or static screenshots built with graphics software. A high-fidelity prototype looks a lot like the real thing and is interactive. This interactivity might be achieved through real coding (hence the need for a front end developer), or through sophisticated use of presentation software like PowerPoint. If instead of a new system, the target of the usability test is an upgrade of an existing system, there should be a test environment or "sandbox" available for testing purposes. This test environment will make very high-fidelity usability testing possible.

Most usability tests are conducted using a series of phases:

1. Planning. This is all the up-front work. The UX researcher is building the usability test script, and is receiving support from business analysts to identify and recruit users. Lab time is booked, if necessary, appointments are placed on participant calendars, a sandbox environment is established for testing the system, etc. For your part, you may be asked to help secure incentives, like a gift card drawing, to help encourage users to participate.

2. Execution. UX researchers are kind of heads-down and alone during this phase, running participants through the usability testing protocol. Realistically, they are also sitting in the lab alone because participants didn't show up to their appointments. They use this time to scramble to try to find replacement participants. Excuses (no lie) run from "My boss pulled me into something critical" to "Lunch went long," and that's if your UX researcher is lucky enough to even be graced with a response. Often, participants just don't show up and don't think a thing of it. Because of this, you may be hearing from your UX researcher for management support like working with other department managers to make sure participants really have time for the sessions and prioritize them.

3. Analysis and Reporting. Once the testing sessions have all been run, the UX researcher has to spend some time going through the data and compiling them. The data might be as simple as notes, but they could also be much more complex - things like timing data, error data, video highlights, eye tracking hotspots, etc. Analysis and reporting complexity varies as well. A usability test report should have, at a minimum:

• Demographics: A quick description of how many users were in your study, along with useful data appropriate to the test: age, sex, business role, customer type, etc.

• Overview of tasks: The audience should be given a feeling of what kinds of things the users did in the test.

• Overview of issues: What went wrong with the UI? What went right? How serious are the issues the researcher found?

A complex study may warrant a 20-page Word document full of tables, statistics, and mockups of proposed solutions. A simpler study may be a 5-slide PowerPoint with an Executive Summary and a few slides about users and issues. At this point you may need to help your UX researcher shape his or her findings so that they're presentable to the intended audience. A VP is not going to read a 20-page document, so you may need to help pick out salient points that make a good 5-minute presentation. You should also be on the lookout for usability test reports that are really something else in disguise.

From the This Really Happened Files:
A colleague of mine was being moved from one project to another, and I was asked to fill in for him on his original project. He sent me his files, which included the results of a usability test. This was encouraging, because a previous usability test can be a valuable baseline for the next round of testing if you know how long tasks typically take, which tasks are especially troubling for users, and what solutions have already been recommended to the Business and development teams. Optimism turned to disappointment, however, when I looked at the "usability test" report. Although it did contain a demographics section outlining which users were contacted, it had no tasks and no objective findings. Each of the slides was full of quotes from users about the system. There was no real usability test conducted - what had occurred was a series of interviews with users to get their impressions, e.g. likes and dislikes, about the system. That kind of study has its place and can be useful, but calling it a usability test was deceptive. The label "usability test" carries a certain weight in the UX world as it's one of the more rigorous and objective approaches to understanding users. Calling an interview report a usability test report was at best careless and worst professionally irresponsible. As a manager you need to have high expectations of your researchers in this regard. If they're saying they're conducting a

usability test, and spending weeks and lots of money doing it, you need to see things like tasks and objective findings in the report.
/End of File

There are several kinds of usability testing, and different terms get thrown around. Some of the earliest forms of usability testing are summative and formative tests. Summative testing gives an impression of the overall usability of a product and is usually conducted on a complete, working system. This often serves as a benchmark for future comparisons. Formative usability testing is more iterative and fits in nicely with Agile development cycles where smaller sections of a system can be prototyped, tested, and provide feedback to the next phase.

Discount usability engineering and testing (Nielsen, 1993) is a reaction to the criticism that usability testing is too time-consuming and expensive, and that there's really no need to run enough participants to get a sample that's truly representative of the population. Instead, you can run a test with five to eight participants and discover most of the usability issues in your system. Beyond that you'll start to see diminishing returns. The idea is to run a test quickly and relatively cheaply, get the issues documented and over to development, and get ready to test in the next development cycle, sprint, etc.

Guerrilla usability testing usually refers to doing away with the entire "user recruitment" component and just grabbing people off the street. Or maybe at a coffee shop. Or at the campus cafeteria. Have them try out a website, or a mobile app, or whatever for few minutes and see what they think. Along with the positives of being inexpensive, quick, and having low resource intensity, there are several negatives with this approach. The most dangerous is the lack of generalizability. In a more formal test, the UX researcher is carefully constructing a sample that is representative of the population. This way the findings of the test can be generalized beyond the sample to the larger population of users. If the system being tested is meant for three different roles in the Procurement department, it's not going to be a smart study design to recruit random people at lunch.

All of these testing methods are valid and have their place. As a manager, however, you need to be aware of the fact that your UX researchers should be capable of testing at all of these levels. If your researcher is insisting that guerrilla usability testing is always the way to go, citing cost effectiveness and so on, that's a big red flag. No real UX researcher is only able to conduct guerrilla usability testing.

From the This Really Happened Files:
I was helping one of my company's suppliers make their user interfaces more usable by our own employees. This supplier was an enterprise software company - they provided big, mainframe-style applications to help business run. Think things like accounting, customer relationship management, purchasing, and supply chain management. They were relatively new to user experience and usability testing, and our two companies were trying to learn how to collaborate on some serious usability issues with their software. My company's users were very frustrated with this supplier's user interface, finding it confusing and awkward. It took too many steps to get anything done, error messages were incomprehensible, and people got lost in the navigation structure all the time. Part of this collaboration involved me observing their usability test sessions. They had a pretty good setup, with a real dedicated lab and researchers going through what looked like proper protocols: open-ended questions, structured tasks, asking the participants to think aloud, good note-taking, etc. The trouble was, things were going *too* well. The participants were cruising through their tasks, the clumsy UI not hindering their progress at all. The researchers were feeling pretty good after demonstrating that their software was not so difficult after all, but they weren't really learning anything. Eventually I just had to ask: Where were these users coming from? Short answer: *the hallway*. The lead researcher said they were ac-

tually just pulling people from their own company into usability test sessions. To their credit he had attempted to match the users' roles with the software, so they weren't testing an accounting UI with Technical Support Representatives, but still this was a software company that used its own software. The problem with their UI was fundamental, not specific to a particular role. Bringing people in to test a version of the software they live and breathe every day, have been trained on and have gotten used to, isn't a recipe for learning how your customers are going to respond. All it gives you is a big dose of confirmation bias. When I pointed out this problem with their approach, they said using their own employees was their only resource and there was no way to get external users. So essentially this company had begun its UX journey by getting all the pieces in place except the most important: UX, or Usability Engineering, or User-Centered Design, is about your *end users*. It is not about just any users, or representatives of those users, or pseudo-users like people you happen to know. If you don't (or can't) know your real end users, don't even bother trying to do UX because you'll just be fooling yourself.

/End of File

Your role in all of this

Two of the most important things you can do from a management perspective when it comes to usability testing is securing authorization and helping with the participant list. One of the major roadblocks your researcher is likely to encounter comes in the form of things like "Those users' time is too valuable to spend in a test session." In these situations it's important to remember the basic value proposition of UX. This is discussed elsewhere in this book, but boils down to investing some time now results in much more time saved later. After you've helped get the test up and running with the OK from upper management (if needed) and making sure participants can actually attend, you should sit in on one of the usability test sessions as an observer. Not only will you be able to see first hand where users have trouble, you can relate this experience to others later to help influence changes in the UI. Down the line, after the test report has been generated, you can help get it in front of the right stakeholders and decision makers by putting together a meeting where the researcher can present the results. Otherwise, all the time and effort put into the research might be wasted by sitting on a hard drive somewhere and not helping influence design.

Research: Heuristic Evaluation

Heuristic evaluation is a kind of expert review pioneered by Jakob Nielsen (1993). Instead of running a system by a bunch of participants, in a heuristic evaluation the UX researcher (or preferably researchers) goes through the system and compares its features and behaviors to a set of heuristics. These heuristics are things like "Error prevention", as it is better to design a UI that prevents errors in the first place rather than addressing errors with warnings (or not at all). If a heuristic is violated, for example if a system does not attempt to prevent user errors, the researcher would mark that as an issue to be addressed and assign it a severity rating and a recommendation for how to solve the issue in a manner that is best for the users. Typically ratings are things like "cosmetic" if it's just something visual that can be quickly changed, and "severe" if the system does something catastrophic like erase a user's data. A heuristic evaluation report is a compilation of these issues and their severity, which can then be transcribed into a project's issue tracker, bug list, etc. For the sake of efficiency, it's best that the evaluation report be a reporting of exceptions - things that are issues to be addressed. I once saw an evaluation report that listed every heuristic for every system feature under consideration. It was 99% "passed", with only two issues reported in a fifteen-page document. That's a ridiculous signal-to-noise ratio, and nobody (especially project stakeholders) is going to want to wade through pages and pages of nothing to find the two things that need to be addressed. Maybe it was meant to make the developers feel good about their system, maybe it was to make the researcher look like he had done more than identify only two issues, I don't know. If there is a valid reason for such a style of report, e.g., you want to make sure your researcher is "showing his work," please also insist on an Executive Summary at the beginning that will save interested parties valuable time.

A major drawback of heuristic evaluations is that, despite being performed by an expert in Human-Computer Interaction (hopefully), they are still subjective. The results one researcher gives you will probably not exactly match those that another researcher will give you. One way to mitigate this is with multiple evaluation efforts, after which the researchers involved get together and agree on the most important issues to address. Another way is to introduce a quantitative aspect to the evaluation. I recently modified heuristic evaluation to include aspects of cognitive modeling based on a version of the GOMS (Goals, Operators, Methods, and Selection rules) model developed by Card, Moran, and Newell (1983). This Keystroke Level Model (KLM) predicts how long a user will take to accomplish a task based on known parameters, e.g., how long it takes to mentally prepare for an action, how long it takes to type a character, how long it takes to move the hands to a device, etc. A purported drawback to this kind of modeling is that it assumes expert performance; the modeled user floundering through an unfamiliar interface is not simulated. This makes it a good match for heuristic evaluation, where expert usage of the existing system (with issues) can be compared with expert usage of a recommended system. The two models are compared side-by-side, providing visual and numeric indicators of how much time could be saved by taking the researcher's advice and implementing the recommended fix. In the figure below, two models built with CogTool software (2015) show how the recommended solution takes less than half the time of the current solution. It also shows how the current solution taxes working memory (the colored stack along the bottom of the chart).

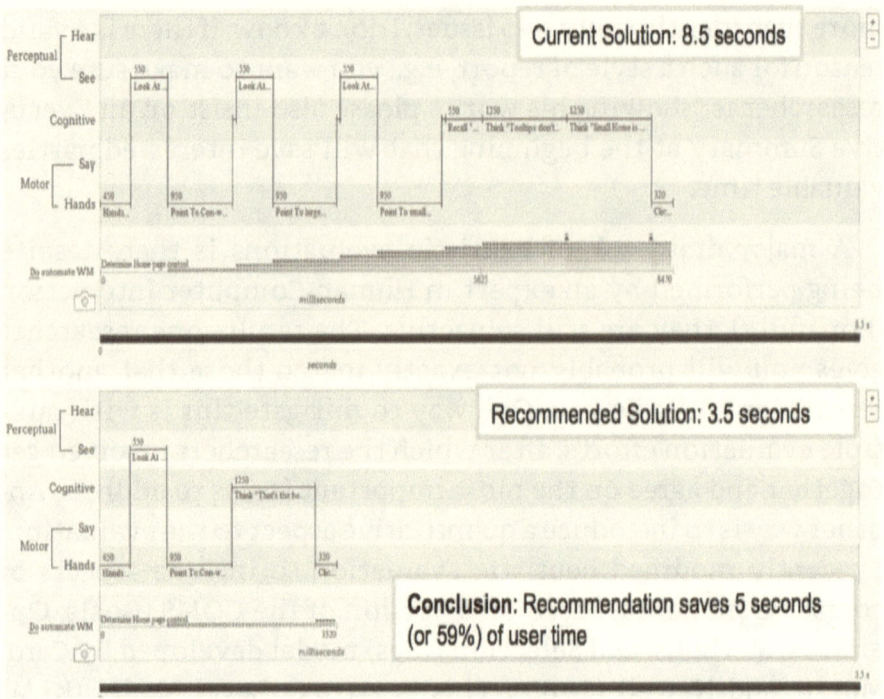

If your researchers are having trouble convincing Business and development teams that their recommended fixes are the way to go, have them look into this technique to add quantitative evidence to their case.

Your role in all of this

Heuristic Evaluation is often a heads-down activity where you won't see much from your UX researcher for a while. It doesn't require much in the way of funding or convincing higher management of its value because it is relatively low-cost. Where you really need to participate is in making sure that the evaluation report isn't simply thrown over the wall to the developers. It needs to be presented in a project team meeting so everyone is made aware of the issues and recommendations, with proper logging into the project's issue tracker. At an even more basic level, you need to make sure that the evaluation report makes sense.

From the This Really Happened Files:

A project manager I'd worked with in the past approached me and said he wanted me to review the work of a new contractor who was doing UX work for him. He said she'd done a heuristic evaluation and it wasn't what he was expecting. I took a look and what I saw was downright weird. It started out with a description of the system under evaluation, which is normal, and a description of the logic of heuristic evaluation. This is also normal, since it can't be assumed that every reader of the report has seen one of these before. But after that is where it got strange. It just kept going, talking about heuristic evaluation, on and on. In the section ostensibly meant for the discussion of issues, it mentioned the enterprise software system under consideration but it was all out of context. It looked like a cut-and-paste job, with the system name substituted for something else. I took a sample of the text and searched for it online, and sure enough found a match. It was from a different company's website where they discussed a heuristic evaluation of their own product. This contractor had written a reasonable introduction to her report, and essentially plagiarized the rest. She would have gotten away with it too, if it hadn't been for a project manager who had had experience with real evaluations and come to me with his concerns. This example is an outlier - I've never seen its equal before or since - but it underscores the need for reviewing of results.
/End of File

Research: Task Analysis

Task Analysis is an umbrella term that covers lots of activities that have one thing in common: understanding what users actually *do* with a system. From your researcher's perspective there are different levels of analysis that are important, e.g., job analysis vs. workflow analysis. What we are most concerned with here is the lower level process and output from these techniques.

Contextual Inquiry and Interviewing

I've grouped these two together not because they're the same thing but because the deliverables are very similar. Interviewing is pretty self-explanatory: The researcher recruits users and talks to them about the system. There is usually a planned script, for example after introductions participants will give a job description, then an overview of their workday, and then tell how the system under investigation is used for accomplishing their goals. Highlights, pain points, and quotes make up the bulk of the report. Interviewing is effective both in person and over the phone or video teleconference.

Contextual inquiry is a bit different. The 'context' in contextual inquiry is the user's workplace - the researcher observes and interacts with the user in the context of her work environment. That means user recruitment, plus extra budget and travel arrangements to reach them, and the researcher should be spending at least an hour with each user. The idea is to get a holistic picture of the users and their systems and workplace together. For example, if there's a physical calculator on a user's desk that he uses for calculations while using your system, that's a problem. The big computer in front of him should be able to handle calculations easily without relying on a totally separate system (in this case the calculator and the user's working memory). This is also the kind of detail that would likely be missed during a phone interview.

The output from these types of activities will consist of raw notes about the users, but the end deliverables will need to be more refined. Expect your researchers to spend more than a week coding the data and building a report. This means going through their notes and looking for themes. This way, as opposed to a big pile of notes with things like "User #1 said the system's keyword search is not working," "User #2 couldn't find 'laptop' using search," and "User #3 successfully found 'notebook' in the purchasing system," the report will highlight that the search function is a high-level issue that needs attention. The details found in the notes may help diagnose the exact issue, but that's best saved for design meetings later.

Procedural Analysis

Sometimes it's helpful to build a diagram of what users typically do in their jobs. A procedural analysis or map is such a diagram, and they're best constructed after direct observations of multiple users carrying out their tasks. Take a look at the following phone conversation between a researcher and a user:

R: Please tell me what you do in your job at the start of the day.
U: I start by checking my email and then using the XR-35 system to order the materials we need for construction.
R: What kind of materials?
U: Lumber, fasteners, nails, and screws.
R: Every day? Every morning?
U: Pretty much. We have to have a constant supply for our workers.

Compare this to an observation session with the same user and researcher:
R: Please show me what you do in your job at the start of the day.
U: Okay. *Opens XR-35 system. Picks up the phone, listens to voicemail, jots a note down. Goes to XR-35 system and order toilet paper. Opens email program and scans the inbox.*
R: Why did you order toilet paper?
U: Someone left me a voicemail that we were out of it again. It happens all the time. It's kind of a priority; I try to take care of stuff like that before getting to the business stuff.

Often when someone instructs a user to "Tell me what you do in your job," they'll skip right to what they think is most pertinent. In an observation-based procedural analysis these missing details get captured, as do other workers involved in the process.

45

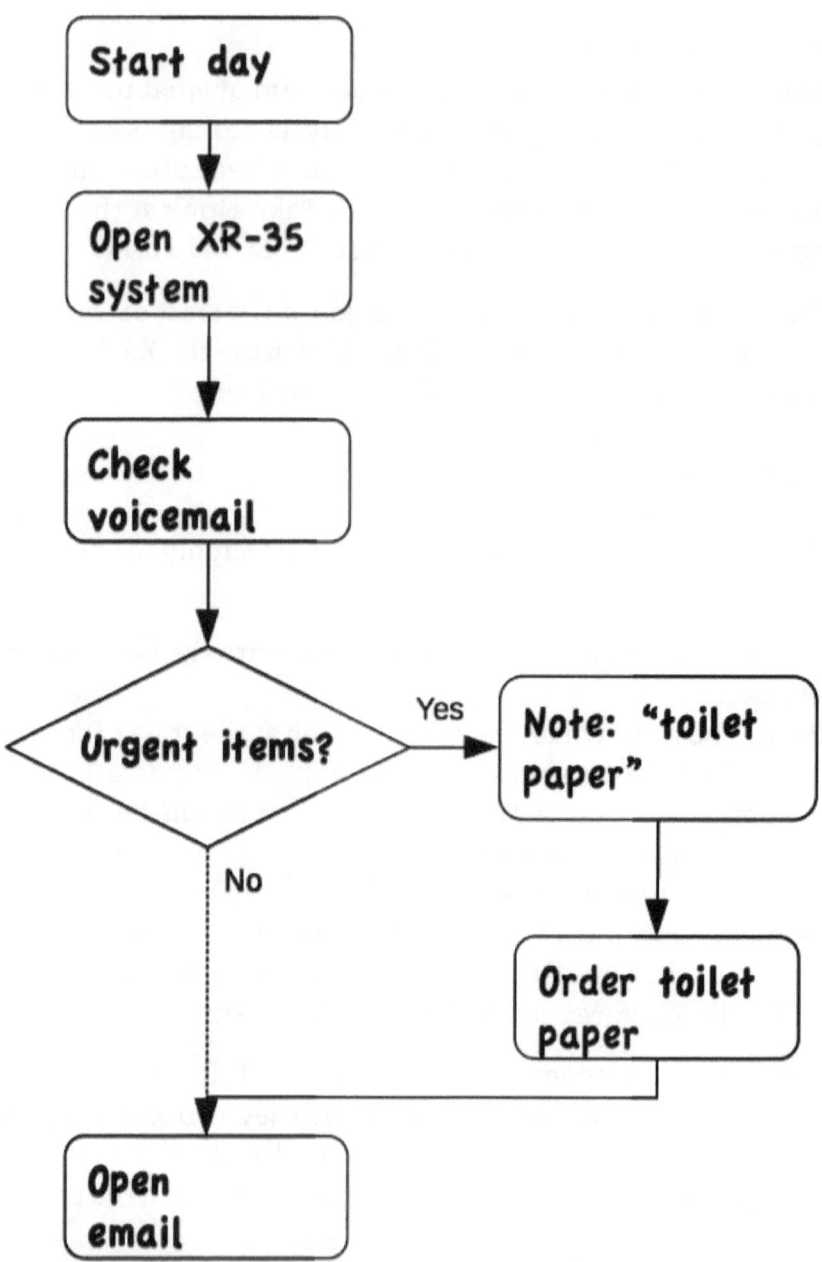

What you don't want to see as a deliverable is a procedural analysis that is nothing but a graphic representation of the business process. That's just a business process map, an idealized flow of how workers and work interact. "The map is not the territory"

- don't mistake a model of how users *should* use the system for the reality of what they actually do. Not only will you not learn anything from such a model, it's possible the researcher is simply being lazy, copying an existing business process map and passing it off as the result of research.

There are other types of mappings, such as task sequences and task hierarchies (Hackos and Redish, 1998), customer journeys, experience maps, and empathy maps. A procedural analysis reflects a low level of detail, which is why it's getting special attention here as it reflects the expertise of the researcher. Raw procedural analyses from individual sessions may be roughly sketched out with a pencil during a study session, or built out of sticky notes. They should include all the things the users actually do while using the system, including errors, sidetracks, and workarounds.

Your role in all of this

Task Analysis is best done one-on-one, in person. Funding and travel arrangements for the UX researcher will be your primary contribution. Recruitment of users, as with other activities, is best facilitated by business analysts. Maybe you know some?

Research: Surveys

At times you may want a standardized measure of how usable a system is so it can be compared to another system. Or, you may want to get as much feedback about a system as possible and usability testing or interviewing is just not going to give you enough data. That's where usability surveys come in. There are two basic kinds of surveys you'll want to become familiar with: General UX Surveys and Usability Scales.

General UX Surveys

These surveys are designed to gather a lot of formative information quickly. They may have a mix of qualitative and quantitative items aimed at understanding user needs and system issues. They can be standalone surveys, done just once at the beginning of a design effort, or they can be done after every release, or on a timed cadence like an annual "Voice of the Customer" survey. A general UX survey may consist of things like:

- Open-ended items, e.g., "Tell us what you think about our website"
- Focused text items, e.g., "What are your top 3 pain points with this system?"
- Likert items, e.g., "Our website's page loads quickly (Strongly Agree | Agree | Somewhat Agree | Neutral | Somewhat Disagree | Disagree | Strongly Disagree)"
- Numerical rating items, e.g., "Please rate our Help Desk service from 1 to 10"

These types of surveys require a lot of analysis because they're not standardized and usually require meticulous coding of the text responses into something meaningful. This is not something that lends itself well to shortcuts. Consider word clouds, which are a popular way of visualizing the frequency of certain words. Imagine a UX survey with an open-ended item about what people disliked about a system. The researcher collects the text data and throws it into a word cloud generator, and shows you this:

The Manager's UX Survival Guide

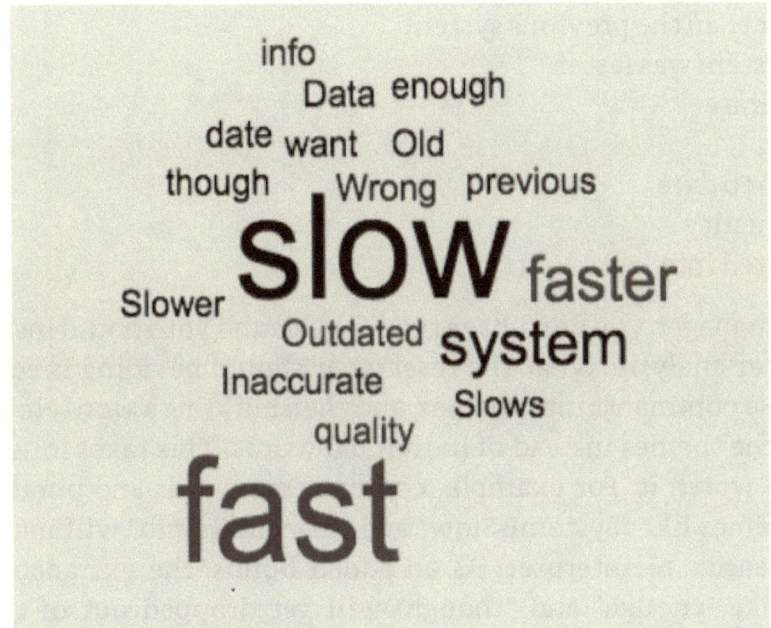

Source: Worditout.com

The problem is immediately apparent. If you see a word cloud like this, send it back - it's undercooked. Now, this is a very simple example without many issues. Still, how do you make sense of this? Is the system slow, or is it fast? How does the standalone word "Data" inform your business decisions? It may help to look at the raw comments from users that went into the cloud:
• Should be fast
• Why isn't it fast
• Not fast though
• Too slow
• Very slow
• Slow
• So slow
• Too slow
• Not fast enough
• I want it to be fast
• Slows me down
• Should be faster

- Slower than the previous system
- Old system was faster
- Inaccurate
- Wrong
- Not up to date
- Data quality
- Outdated info

As a manager, you don't have time for this and you should insist on better analysis. What the researcher should be doing is coding these comments into themes, and then building a word cloud out of the themes instead of individual words. This takes longer but it's worth it. For example, coding these words and phrases into themes like "SystemIsSlow" and "InaccurateInfo" will make things easier to interpret. As an added bonus, the extraneous noise like "enough" and "though" will get dropped out of the cloud. Here's a revised version with more up-front analysis done:

Source: Worditout.com

This *looks* less impressive at first glance because all those different ways of saying that the system isn't fast enough have been distilled into a common theme, and in this unrealistic example only two issues emerge. It's a lot more useful than the first meaningless cloud, which has more visual pop, but doesn't actually say anything. This illustrates an underlying principle of surveying: If the output of a survey doesn't give you actionable insights, it's a waste of time.

Usability Scales

For a more quantitative and comparative approach, a usability scale is the way to go. The idea of a usability scale is to get a numeric score for an application or system that allows it to be compared to:
- Another application
- A previous version of the same application (Version 2 vs. Version 1)
- A predetermined benchmark (e.g., 80 out of 100)

The SUS, or System Usability Scale (Brooke, 1996), is a popular way to measure usability on a scale of 1 to 100. It is a scale with 10 statements where Strongly Disagree is a one and Strongly Agree is a five. It takes each participant just a few minutes to answer, so it's a good choice to distribute to a large sample.

I developed an alternative to the SUS called the Usability Metric for User Experience, or UMUX (Finstad, 2010b). It gives a 1 to 100 score comparable to the SUS using four items on a 7-point agree/disagree scale. Part of my motivation for developing the UMUX was to avoid some language issues I found with the SUS (Finstad, 2006), and I wanted to use 7-point scales after finding they are more sensitive than 5-point scales (Finstad, 2010a). What really makes it effective, however, is that it takes less than half the time of the SUS for each participant to complete, which makes it an easier sell when pitching a survey to upper management. If you're starting up a UX department and your researchers aren't experts in a particular scale, the UMUX is very easy to implement, especially in online survey tools. The survey items are:

1. [This system] meets my requirements.
2. Using [this system] is a frustrating experience.
3. [This system] is easy to use.
4. I have to spend too much time correcting things with [this

system].

Substitute whatever you're studying in place of [this system] and provide a 1-7 scale with "Strongly Disagree" as the label for 1 and "Strongly Agree" as the label for 7. None of the other numbers have labels. The scoring requires some special attention because they're phrased in a way to keep people paying attention – the odd numbered items are phrased positively, and the even numbered items are phrased negatively. To get their scores all pointing in the same positive direction, some transformation is needed. First, subtract one from the odd items' scores. This makes their range zero to six instead of one to seven. If Item #1 scored a six, it then becomes a five (leaning in the positive direction for meeting requirements). For the even numbered items, subtract the score from seven. This also provides for a zero-to-six transformation. If Item #2 scored a two, it becomes a five after being subtracted from seven. This is the mathematically positive interpretation of disagreeing that the system is frustrating (which is a good thing). Add up all four items, divide by 24, and multiply by 100. That will give you a 0 – 100 score for that respondent. Here's a full example of how the scoring works for a respondent:

UMUX Item	Raw: 1 to 7	Recode: 0 to 6
1	6	5
2	2	5
3	5	4
4	1	6
		Sum: 20
		÷ 24: .833
		x 100: **83.3**

Repeat this for all respondents and average their scores and you will have your overall UMUX score for the system. This is what it all boils down to: while the core deliverable from a general UX survey is a breakdown of themes that emerged, a usability scale like this is focused on the score. I've built a UMUX analyzer that screens survey data, does the recoding and calculating, and pro-

The Manager's UX Survival Guide

vides a graphic that can be placed in a report. Since the UMUX is designed to match the System Usability Scale, the scoring scale is a modified version of one from Bangor, Kortum, and Miller (2008). The final result looks like this:

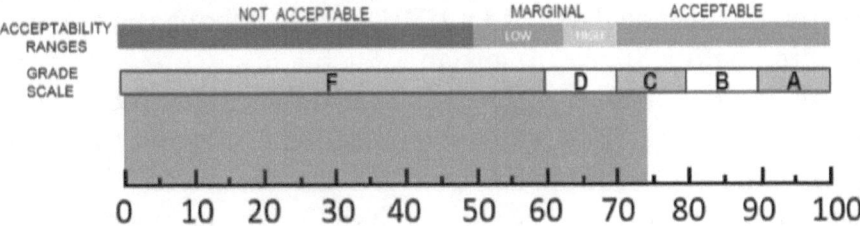

A usability scale survey report doesn't need much more than this. It's a straightforward measure that shows that, in this case, an application scoring 74/100 can be deemed "Acceptable," but there's room for improvement. A future version would hopefully be getting up into the B or A grade ranges.

It's important to remember that both the UMUX and SUS are *standardized scales*, meaning that they are valid and reliable instruments as long as you don't change them. I can't count the number of times I've heard of people wanting to change the wording of an item here, another there, etc. If you allow that, you can still get a score, but it won't be comparable to other systems you've run UMUX or SUS on in the past, or all the other applications out there in the world you'd like to use as a measuring stick.

It's also important to note that a standardized scale score is a metric, not a diagnostic tool. There are diagnostic surveys out there, but they take a long time for each participant to complete and that's going to be a hard sell to stakeholders when one of the primary selling points of surveys like this is low impact to their users' time. What I usually do is include two open-ended items about what users like and dislike most about the system after the numeric rating portion. Once properly analyzed (see the above word cloud example) you can get to a nice starting point for improving the UX of your system.

From the This Really Happened Files:

Kraig Finstad

I was in charge of the UX component of a department-wide effort to rate and improve the quality of our internal systems. One of the first apps to be rated was a mobile café menu app that allowed employees to look up what their local site's café was serving during the day. I did a UMUX survey about the app and it scored below 50, earning it an F. Such a low score warranted a more serious look, but the project team's first instinct was to blame the *survey*. They said it was inaccurate, the sampling must be wrong, people couldn't understand the items – anything and everything but admit that the app itself might have a problem. Its performance was fine – everything loaded quickly and it conformed to UI standards, had responsive design, etc. When I did the comment analysis it quickly emerged that people disliked the app because it was often wrong. People would look up the menu, plan on having a certain item at lunch, and then in the café itself they'd find it wasn't being served. It was ultimately a data quality issue that profoundly affected the user experience. Once a firm business process was put in place to align the menu with the real world, the UX issue disappeared and so did criticisms about the UMUX itself. The app re-tested in the A grade range, and the UMUX was then seen as a really good instrument. Not just because it was telling people what they wanted to hear, but because at first it told them something they hated to hear, and then faithfully reflected the change in users' attitudes once the issue was addressed. This helped build trust with the survey process.
/**End of File**

Statistical Analysis

Both standardized scales and general UX surveys can pull in data appropriate for complex statistical analysis. This is a touchy subject, because statistics is one of those areas where people often have just enough knowledge to be dangerous. Statistical methods are very easy to misapply, and modern computer software makes analysis look a lot easier than it really is. If a researcher doesn't really understand the fundamentals, there's a danger that their findings could be spurious and lead to poor business decisions. Statistics can be done on all kinds of UX Research, but surveys are the most common, which is why it's being discussed here. All of your UX researchers should understand basic statistical concepts like means, standard deviations, and frequency distributions. These are called "descriptive statistics" and do exactly that - they are ways of describing the data. Excel is more than sufficient for finding the mean of a dataset, calculating a standard deviation, or plotting a simple graph. Where it gets complicated is with inferential statistics. These are techniques where the findings from a sample are generalized to a population. To complicate matters, there are different levels of measurement, parametric and nonparametric techniques, univariate and multivariate techniques, etc. You don't have to worry about the details, but one main concept to become familiar with in this realm is statistical significance. Briefly, if a finding (such as the error rate on System A being lower than that of System B) is unlikely to be due to chance, it is said to be statistically significant. Researchers use this significance criterion to demonstrate that their finding is likely reflected in the real world, in the target population, and isn't just a fluke. The formulations of "System A has the same error rate as System B" and "System A has a different error rate from System B" are two types of hypotheses to be tested. This is the proper way to put a user experience experiment together. Going in with no hypotheses and testing every data comparison possible is called a "fishing expedition" and is the sign of a poor researcher.

From the This Really Happened Files:

My org's principal researcher was in charge of a User Voice type survey, where thousands of our company's employees were sent a 20-minute survey about how the IT department was doing. It didn't use a standardized usability scale, but did use satisfaction ratings. Anything above a neutral on the scale was considered "Satisfied", and percentages of satisfied users were calculated across all of the company's different divisions and geographies. This was a very large data set that could be sliced and diced in pretty much any way you could imagine. The results were brought into a department meeting *after* they had already been shown to higher management. Uh oh. No worries though! The principal researcher had included a newly hired "data guy" to help out with analysis. Data Guy was really more of a Data*base* Guy, though, more proficient in SQL than in statistics. They put up a big column graph showing the satisfaction percentages for 20 different departments, and for the most part they were positive. 63% satisfied here, 68% satisfied there, 64.5% satisfied over there...There was nothing inherently wrong with this, it was just a description of what they found. Where it went wrong was when the principal researcher proudly proclaimed, "And these are all statistically significant differences!"

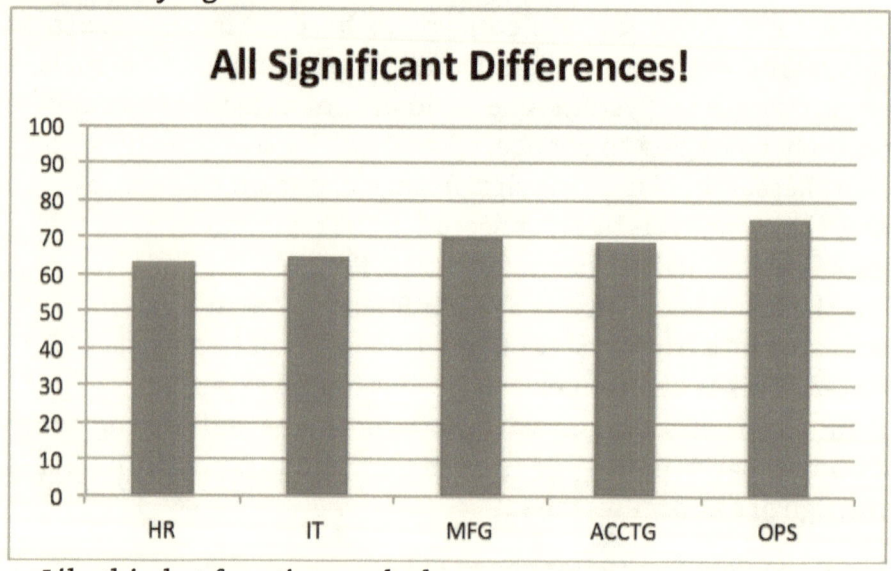

Like this, but four times as bad

This was an odd claim for many reasons. I asked, "What are they significantly different from?" The answer came back, "From each other." There's a red flag. I looked at the graph again and asked, "So you found that 63% is significantly different from 64.5%?" Again, the answer came back in the affirmative. I didn't know what to say. They had messed this up so badly, and had taken it to higher

management without proper peer review when they had *actual statisticians on staff*...First of all, the claim that all the different departments were significantly different from each other was just plain incorrect. The more comparisons you do, the tighter and tighter the criterion for significance gets and you have to report what this margin is, and that wasn't done here. Second, and more crucially, *so what?* How are these findings actionable? It doesn't help you make business decisions if 63% versus 75% is significant but so is 63% versus 64.5%. If everything is significant, *nothing is*.
/End of File

Statistical significance has its place, such as being able to show that the new version of a system is actually easier to use than the old version, or easier than a competitor's version. A quantitative finding needs to be backed up with a solid explanation of what the finding actually means. Be aware that statistically significant does not necessarily mean *important*. You wouldn't be surprised to find that admins are significantly faster at setting up conference calls than developers, and you're not going to invest thousands of dollars closing that gap. What you should be surprised at is that the researcher went on such a ridiculous fishing expedition in the first place.

Your role in all of this

Surveys are a lighter-touch activity compared to things like usability testing and contextual inquiry; you're only asking for a few minutes of time from each participant. The pushback you do receive from higher management will often take the form of privacy concerns. Make sure everyone involved (upper management, researchers, business analysts who are helping recruit, etc.) understands that responses need to be *at least* confidential, and ideally be made anonymous. Feedback cannot be traced back to individuals, despite arguments like "We're all part of the same company" and "I need to know which one of my people said that." Due to these concerns, it's helpful to have researchers with backgrounds where they've been trained for years on privacy and confidentiality (like psychology). As for statistics, please refer to the Interview Guide at the end of this book to help sort through candidates that will be able to do them right.

Research: Personas

You've probably heard of personas. Not because they're the most effective methods from UX Research, but because they're highly visual, distributable, and consumable. They're also relatively easy to put together, and easy to get wrong. A persona is a kind of "archetypal user" that gives Design and development a face and personality to stand in for that dry stuff like usability issues and statistics. Imagine stock photos of "Allan the Accountant" or "Penny the Purchaser," along with job descriptions and lists of what Allan and Penny need to do their jobs.

Some departments go all-in on personas. Big posters of Allan and Penny get printed out and put in hallways, conference rooms, and cubicle walls. They're treated as if they were real people in meetings. "Well, how will your design change affect Allan's workflow?" Some departments only give them lip service: Allan and Penny appear in a PowerPoint slide deck summarizing 6 months of user research and are never seen again by most of the project team. They become, if they're lucky, part of the development process as UX Research and UX Design collaborate. If you experiment with personas and find that higher management likes them and wants to see them play a role in your UX org's identity, great. What's more important here is differentiating useful, effective personas from useless pseudo-personas.

From the This Really Happened Files:

My organization decided to go all-in on personas. A small team of researchers was put together to not only build personas, but assemble them into a series of "trading cards" - small, laminated summaries of different hypothetical users. The marketing aspect was kicked off at an internal UX conference where everyone received a set of these cards. We were encouraged to mill around and trade with others for cards we didn't have. It was essentially

an ice-breaker exercise that was over in ten minutes. After the conference, mention of the trading cards popped up now and again because they made it into team status reports and it was rumored that certain executives liked them. Where they weren't seen was design meetings or deeper research studies. Several months of effort, thousands of dollars in printing and promotion, and no impact to the actual end users in terms of improved systems. All that effort and money expended on a little bit of team building.
/End of File

Personas need to have actionable information. Their utility is extremely limited as an empathy-builder. Some purists may say personas should be like real descriptions of people, but a useful persona should have some information about how hypothetical the hypothetical user really is. How much time per day is a real worker wearing this persona as a "hat"? What percentage of these people experience a known usability issue? Without actionable information, personas like Allan and Penny just end up in a drawer with last year's conference lanyard.

Your role in all of this

Don't settle for pseudo-personas and keep in mind that personas are supposed to help keep the design and development process on track. If a researcher produces personas as part of a project, look beyond the fancy graphics and ask yourself (and the researcher) "What do I do with this?" You've heard about lying with statistics? It's even easier to lie with personas. A persona with no numbers or facts could just be a dreamed-up "ideal user" the researcher has put together based on a couple interviews, or even just assumptions.

User Interface Design

Remember back in the Common Sense Guide to User Experience, how I teased the idea that a great UI is the product of inspiration and experience? To have a great design, you have to have a great designer. Doesn't get more common sense than that. Back then, when I pointed out that that notion is a bunch of baloney, I alluded to what the real story is. But I shouldn't have to – by now it should be obvious, with all this talk of understanding users through UX Research, that a great design is a product of a process, of effort, combined with talents from many fronts.

One of my hobby interests is the Shakespeare Authorship Question. There's a debate among academics and enthusiasts about whether the man we know as William Shakespeare, a glover's son from Stratford-upon-Avon, is the true author of immortal works like Hamlet and Macbeth. Those who believe he was are called Stratfordians, after "the man from Stratford." Those on the other side of the debate, the Anti-Stratfordians, believe that "William Shakespeare" is a pseudonym used by someone who wanted his identity as a playwright concealed (in those days writing plays was seen as pedestrian and contemptible by polite society). One of the most powerful arguments on the Anti-Stratfordian side is that some of the works of Shakespeare are from sources that were not translated into English in the 1600s, and there is no evidence of Shakespeare having any sort of formal education (although there are endless conjectures and extrapolations regarding his education in biographies) or travel abroad. The Stratfordian answer is dismissive: William Shakespeare was an unparalleled genius, and his genius allowed him to simply *know* these sources, and classical sources like Ovid, and the intricacies of Italian daily life and French courtly life, without having to read about them or experience them first-hand. If this kind of argument makes sense to you, you might have an alternate career path as a Shakespeare academic, but please discontinue your UX management journey because you're destined to fail if you think you can hire a 'genius' UX designer who can magically understand user needs without having any research done. Besides, any such genius should be applying his or her monumental talents on world-changing efforts, not an accounting system.

With that out of the way, I'm not going to spend a lot of time on UI Design because it's arguably the most tangible, obvious output from the user experience process. Everyone knows about user interfaces, and improving user interfaces is usually seen as the whole point of UX. In fact, a major goal of this book is to help you recognize that a great user interface is *not* just the product of a designer at his stand-up desk and MacBook Pro. As a manager or project manager, you shouldn't have too much difficulty convincing the higher-ups that your system is going to need a user interface, and you might as well go ahead and make a good one. That's an easy sell. The hard sell is convincing them that a lone, albeit talented, Designer is not enough. Even then, once your UX Design capacity is in place and going about its business, it's OK to look at its output with a critical eye.

From the This Really Happened Files:

I was on a UX team that would do peer reviews from time to time, to get a second set of eyes on what UX deliverables were being developed on other projects. One of my UX colleagues had designed a graphical status system that was supposed to help users understand if the system was working within acceptable tolerances or if attention was required. It took not even a minute of peer review for me to reject his proposal, which consisted of things like:

- Gold (which looked yellow) = Everything's fine. His rationale: "It's gold as in 'Good As Gold.'" Seriously?
- Green = Bad. His rationale: "Green like money, or greed, which is bad." Again, seriously?
- Red = Warning, like an injury (blood). Out of this entire crazy scheme, this one made the most sense, but that's not saying much.

Mind you, this is in a world where traffic signals exist, and it was common in the org to say things like "The project status is yellow light," meaning in danger of falling to the bad red zone. The one solid human factors reason for not using a traffic signal analogy is that some users are color-blind and won't be able to readily distinguish red from green. The solution to that has al-

ways been to double-code the signals with color *and* shape, such as with a green checkmark, yellow triangle with exclamation point, and red "X." He wasn't even leaning on the color-blindness angle – he thought a system of visual-to-verbal analogies could outperform an established system that adult users won't even have to think about. The lesson here is that UX designers can overthink and overdesign things. If a design makes no sense and has to be explained to you, it will probably have to be explained to the end users. If in doubt, have a researcher test it.
/End of File

Trusting the Heavyweights

A big trend in modern UI design is to simply implement a library or design language built by someone else, for example Google's Material Design. The logic here is that all the research and pixel-pushing has already been taken care of, so your org can just plug it in and turn it on! If only it were so easy...there are of course several things to keep in mind with this approach. The first is that the library may simply be a bad match for the system you are trying to design. It may work great on phones, but doesn't scale well to a custom enterprise system. Another problem is that UX designers do more than design icons and controls. All those little widgets need to be put into a coherent screen flow that users will understand and be able to use. Additionally, the big names who designed it might have gotten it wrong, and then where will you be? There has been a trend in recent years towards 'flat' design, which is supposed to be a way of having the UI fade into the background and let the content rule the screen...but mostly it's an exercise in proving that we're not in the 1990s anymore and it's unfashionable to have a button look like a button. What we're ending up with is controls that don't invite any interaction, where the user can't tell if a word is just text or something they can tap or click. I guess the next step is to do away with the graphical UI altogether and go back to green screens of text, only with some words clickable and some not.

Your role in all of this

As a manager or project manager, you have your eye on the complete business. Be skeptical and reasonable with design proposals. In many cases, you'll be able to just accept the UX recommendations and designs, but sometimes you'll have to use your insight into the bigger picture to reject things. For example, if a design violates corporate brand standards, help the UX designers align their work better. Maybe help them understand that a design can't happen now, but together you can work towards changing the standards themselves in the future.

Design: Prototyping

Prototypes are an essential part of a UX designer's world. They can take many forms, but they all serve a similar purpose: provide a test bed for user reactions and behavior. Some prototypes are built alongside screen designs, as a way of testing whether the flow on the screen makes sense. Others are built further down the line, to investigate interactivity. You may have heard of prototypes referred to as being low-fidelity and high-fidelity. Fidelity is determined by how closely the prototype resembles the actual working system in look and feel.

Low-Fidelity prototypes

These types of prototypes are built with a sort of "fail fast" philosophy. Throw something together, don't invest a lot of energy into making it look and feel like a real system, and just see if the basics work. These prototypes are meant to be constructed quickly and taken into usability testing, then reconstructed with learnings from the test. A low-fidelity prototype could be made of paper, it could be series of PowerPoint slides demonstrating a flow through screens, or it could be a clickable wireframe demonstrating some rudimentary interactivity. Here's an example of a wireframe:

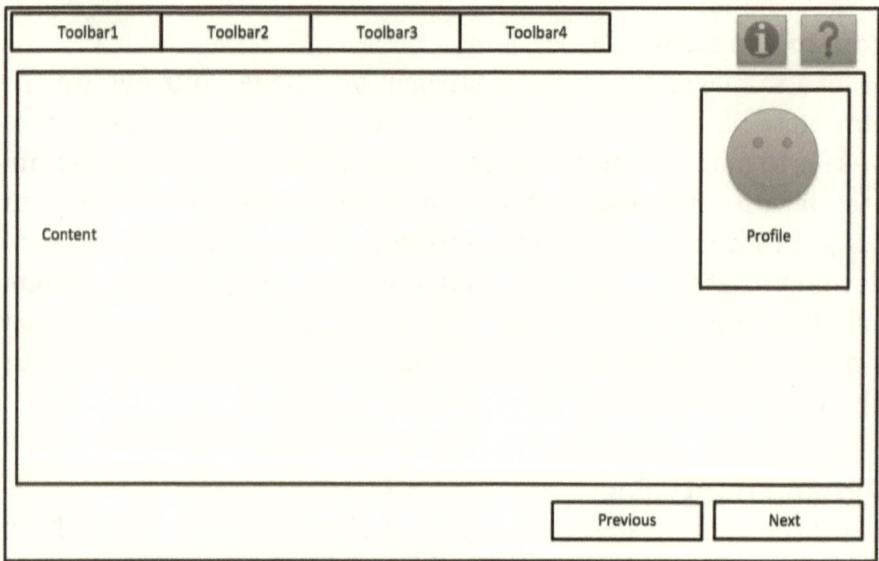

Not much to look at, right? That's intentional. If you see a UX designer building something like this, don't assume they don't have any graphic design skills. These types of prototypes are meant to just get the flow of the screen right without users and stakeholders getting too hung up on details, such as colors and button shapes. That kind of fine-tuning takes a lot of time, and will be added later. Some prototyping tools (like Balsamiq, 2016) have this approach built in, providing clickable sketch-style prototypes that can be built quickly. The whole point is to not spend a lot of time on each prototype/test iteration, so you can do more of them and learn more.

High-Fidelity prototypes

These types of prototypes are meant to demonstrate how on-screen controls actually work, for example to show users what they can expect when they click a button. They also look very complete in terms of design choices, so the screens look like a real system. In fact, they often are real systems! Sandbox environments of enterprise software, for example, make for great high-fidelity prototypes when moving from one version of the software to the next. There are various reasons to invest in high-fidelity prototyping. On the user side, it makes for a more natural interaction where users can behave as they normally would with a system. On the technology side, there are times when the interaction requires a strong back-end presence that is very difficult to simulate with a clickable wireframe. Remember the laptop/notebook problem I alluded to in Chapter 3? Imagine trying out a low-fidelity prototype of a search engine:

Usability Test Administrator: "OK, try to find a pencil using this system."
User: "I'd type 'pencil' into the search box and press the Search button."

Prototype:

```
[ Pencil ]   [ Search ]

Results:
   Pencil
```

Usability Test Administrator: "Is that what you expected to see?"
User: "Yes."
Usability Test Administrator: "Now try to find a notebook computer using this system."
User: "I'd type 'notebook' into search and press Search."
Prototype:

```
[ Notebook ]   [ Search ]

Results:
   Notebook computer
```

Usability Test Administrator: "Is that what you expected to see?"
User: "Yes"

Now, is this realistic at all? No, of course not. Have we learned anything from this usability task? Not really. The only reason the user said he would type 'notebook' is because the administrator used that word in the task description. One step up the causal chain, the only reason the administrator used the word 'notebook' is because she knew in advance that was what the limited prototype was capable of returning. Situations like these are much more appropriate for a high-fidelity prototype that has some real logic behind it to help illuminate actual user behavior, such as a user typing 'laptop' into a search field and getting no hits because only 'notebook' is in the actual, working database. Catching something like the laptop/notebook problem early on where it can be fixed is worth the up-front investment in a high-fidelity prototype.

Your role in all of this

The best thing you can do for your UX designers when it comes to prototyping is defer to their skillsets. If they want to build low-fidelity prototypes using Balsamiq (2016) or something similar, get that software. Don't insist that "PowerPoint is good enough," because it isn't. Your department may already have PowerPoint for everyone's computers already, but it will be a false savings as building prototypes that way will take a *lot* longer and take up a lot of your designer's time. For high-fidelity prototypes, you may need to coordinate with other departments to get a collaboration going with a developer who can help build a working simulacrum.

CHAPTER 6: YOUR UX DEPARTMENT

How big, how many, how much?

Down to brass tacks. How big of an organization do you need? How many UX researchers? How many UX designers? How many UX VPs? It's honestly impossible to say - it depends on the company, and the organization structure within it. I've worked at places where there was a strong UX capability in one line of business and none at all in the others. What I can tell you is that, in general, you should have about the same number of researchers as you have designers. This is because ideally they'll be partners on projects. I will also say that you should make sure you have at least one person for "the hard stuff" on each side of the UX coin. For Research this means having one statistician who can drive usability metrics standards, check others' analyses, and just make sure data are not being deceptively used in general. On the Design side this means one person who can do real Javascript programming (for example) to build screens if you don't have access to a front-end developer.

Beyond that, here are some rules of thumb for putting together your UX organization:
• Don't hire a bunch of UX researchers who specialize in interviewing. If you have to err on the side of a specialization, make it usability testing. Anyone with a solid usability testing background can do interviewing, but the inverse is not true.
• Too many UX researchers will turn the overworked UX designers into a bottleneck.

• Too many UX designers will end up idling while waiting for issues to address from the overworked UX researchers

• Each UX researcher and designer should be spending about 30% - 50% of their time on a particular project. Don't overload them by giving them too many projects as you'll just see diminishing returns. Your researchers need time to figure out the best approaches to a UX problem, and your designers need time to really understand the current interface.

In any case, plan ahead. If your UX capability is brand-new, and is being put together for a particular program (comprising multiple projects), you could start with one researcher and one designer and have them both be on that project for 100% of their billable (non-overhead) time. If you have two programs starting, then hire two researchers and two designers.

Maturing the org

A UX maturity model is a way of thinking about how well UX is integrated into your org or company. An immature org will have little or no UX integration while a mature org will have full integration. People use Apple as an example of a company with a highly integrated UX (or user-centered) culture, meaning that considering the end user is a fully ingrained aspect of everything they do. Another way to think about it is this: if you have user-centered design professionals making recommendations that are constantly dismissed as "too expensive", you don't have a user-centered *organization*, you just have some user-centered *individuals*.

There are plenty of UX maturity models out there, some with just a few levels, some with more. A common metaphor of stairs is used to show both how a company can progress higher and higher, and how one level of maturity is built on top of another.

The Manager's UX Survival Guide

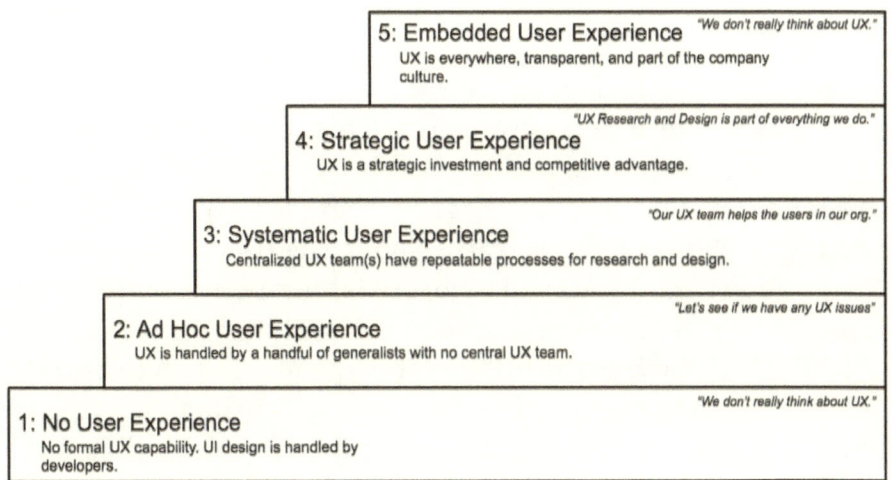

Level 1: No User Experience

At this level people at your company have either never heard of user experience (or usability, or user-centered design) or don't think it's worth the investment. Screen design is handled by developers, and attitudes about your systems are probably investigated by Marketing if they are external, and by nobody if they're internal. Someone may be able to put together an A/B test to determine which screen gets more hits from users, but will not be able to tell you *why* that is happening.

Level 2: Ad Hoc User Experience

At this level there may be a manager or someone with the bright idea to try putting an expert in Human-Computer Interaction somewhere to help design your systems. UX professionals are usually generalists, meaning they do a combination of UX Research and Design. Unfortunately, with so few of them around, their time is heavily taxed and they aren't able to make much of an impact. There's a real danger at this level of your UX resources being pressured to "bless" designs made by others, or to provide a "sanity check" to make sure things were done right. This kind of thinking goes hand-in-hand with the idea that UX is something that's done at the end of the project, and quickly. It's not a recipe for success, but it's a start.

Level 3: Systematic User Experience

Here is where it gets interesting. This level is characterized by one or more centralized UX teams with clear internal roles, like UX researcher and UX designer. There is a structured methodology to how Research learns about the users, then informs Design about user needs and usability issues. Design build prototypes, which in turn Research then tests. This cycle is iterative, with the final, best-performing prototype moving on to be built out by the developers. The efforts are still primarily tactical, however, with the UX resources going after things that regular management wants. There's no high-level UX representative in management (maybe a figurehead "champion" or "advocate" somewhere) guiding the org or company to a place where UX is done end-to-end for all systems. If you can get to this level, great! This will likely feel like a plateau, as it's hard to get beyond Level 3. Whatever happens, though, don't slide back down to a lower level. One thing that can happen is companies can make the mistake of scaling back their UX efforts and fall into a self-fulfilling prophecy by getting rid of the mechanisms for measuring the success of UX in the first place. If you don't have any reliable way of measuring how bad things are, you won't know how bad they've become, right?

Level 4: Strategic User Experience

This is where UX leadership becomes a reality. A visible, attainable UX career ladder is in place, and your UX experts have a clear line of sight to become influencers. There is also a vision for UX, and it is recognized by upper management as being something that contributes to the company's bottom line. Instead of just chasing down usability issues, there is a prescriptive aspect to user experience; i.e., leaders are setting the course for new products and systems that will benefit users, make them more effective and efficient, etc. Make no mistake, though - it is hard to get to this level. Many companies stall out at Level 3 and never reach Level 4. Level 3 is seen as "good enough" and many organizations can't see much past the next quarter's results. Getting to the strategic Level 4 means advocating for a much larger perspective.

Level 5: Embedded User Experience

This is the big one, and it's very, very rare. Truly embedded user experience means that the company doesn't even think about it any more. There may be job roles dedicated to UX, but it's never a question that the UX of a new product or system will be taken care of. Everyone at the company cares about UX, and to not put the user first when starting a new project is unthinkable.

Given all this, do you recognize your own company and where they stand? Wallowing around in the shallow end of this pool is pointless. You're paying people either to (1) waste time recommending changes that will never happen, or (2) lie to you and tell you everything is just super! UX doesn't really start paying off until about Level 3. The good news is that's also the stage where your UX people will start looking to build up the maturity level and advocate for a better career ladder. This is a journey you should be on together.

From the This Really Happened Files:

I had a conversation with a recruiter who was trying to fill a position with a client that was just starting out with UX Research. The client's requirements for the position looked well thought-out, but on closer inspection problems emerged. They wanted someone to do the regular stuff, like conduct usability tests and surveys, collaborate with designers, write reports - the nuts and bolts. So far, so good. I was actually impressed to see that they also wanted this person to develop and test hypotheses. Down the page, though, it turned out they were looking for someone with a Bachelor's degree and 2+ years of experience. A degree in a field where hypothesis testing would be taught, like psychology, was a "plus" and not a requirement. Giving them the benefit of the doubt, perhaps the client was so new to UX Research they didn't know that hypothesis testing requires training in experi-

mental design and statistics and isn't something at which junior researchers will excel.
/End of File

Hopefully this far into the book you can see what's wrong with advertising for a position like this. If your UX capability is brand new, it's OK to start off at the ground level and just get some basic research or design started. It's preferable to bring in an experienced leader who can oversee research projects, design experiments, and do the advanced analysis on data gathered by junior members hired later. It's not a good idea to try to fill a leadership position with an entry-level UXer and hope they can do everything right out of the gate. This will look like saving money to the bean counters, but will cost a lot more in the long run when hypotheses aren't tested at all or are tested incorrectly.

It's going to be even harder for a junior researcher to build a complete UX capability from scratch without much experience in the field. It's going to be up to you to get the right people in place to grow your UX org for success. If you're just starting out, hire a senior person who has a proven track record of improving systems. Make this person a team leader who is responsible for putting together a UX program, but not a people-manager. This team lead will help you develop job descriptions for the lower level positions. This is the first step in establishing an attractive career ladder.

UX Career Ladders

Although they don't appear in the graphics of maturity models, career ladders are actually a fundamental aspect. You can't have a mature organization without good people, and you won't have any good people without a decent career ladder. You may be able to hire them, but they'll be drawn away by better career aspects elsewhere. A full career ladder is motivating and inspiring, a step stool is not. I worked at a company that had a full line of sight all the way up through Principals and on to Fellows for technical positions. Employees could see others paving the way for UX to be a highly valued discipline. Another company had the same "Analyst" job code for all UX roles, although we were allowed to call ourselves "researchers" and "designers." The main problem was that there were a couple Analyst grades and then one Principal grade, of which each org got just one. That means there was no real room for promotion - no matter how good you were, how hard you worked, or how much value you brought to the company, you were stuck at the Analyst level unless that one Principal left and opened up the slot. Very demotivating. Even worse, there was a level above Principal vaguely called "IT Consultant" that was a kind of special appointment position that higher management could hand out but that wasn't attainable any other way. Everyone was just kind of stuck. Only figuratively though - they weren't so stuck that they couldn't quit to pursue better opportunities, which pretty much everyone did.

When you're developing a career ladder to make UX as successful as possible, keep the following factors in mind:

• Visibility: Job roles (and codes) should be clear descriptors, not vague generalizations (like "Analyst")

• Attainability: Don't limit the positions at higher levels to just one person - nothing will short-circuit employee motivation faster than seeing there's nowhere to go but down (or out).

• Merit: Each position higher on the ladder should be achievable by anyone exceeding expectations at their current level. They shouldn't have to have the right connections or play political games (such as undermining their colleagues).

Here's an example of a UX Research career ladder with some notes about what it entails:

UX Technician

This junior team member spends a lot of time in the usability lab testing participants. The usability tests are designed by more senior researchers so the job is purely technical rather than strategic. The technician is provided the usability test script and a list of participants to schedule. The tests are run and recorded and then the data are handed off to the UX researcher in charge of the project. Psychology students usually have some lab experience where they are trained in unbiased data collection from participants, so a bachelor's degree in this field is a good fit for an entry-level UX technician position.

UX Specialist

This role is basically an expanded version of the technician role, for example the above person with their bachelor's degree and one or two years of experience working in the field. Responsibilities can be expanded to include things like interviews, contextual inquiry, and job shadowing. Anthropology students are a good fit here. The data from studies are still handed off to more senior researchers for analysis and reporting.

UX Researcher

At this level some background in Human-Computer Interaction becomes more important, as the UX researcher will be expected to be able to apply all the techniques in the UX Research toolbox. Strong training in usability engineering principles is important for making screen design recommendations and conducting heuristic evaluations. This is also the point in the ladder where the researcher is designing the usability tests, contextual inquiry protocols, etc. and handing them off to the technicians and specialists. UX researchers should also be able to administer basic surveys. Conversely, those roles are handing off their data for basic analysis and reporting by the UX researcher. A master's degree in Human-Computer Interaction is a good starting point for this role, as is the UX specialist role plus several years of experience.

Senior UX researcher

This level of the ladder has a fundamental shift in responsibility. Instead of focusing on the project or system level, a senior UX researcher is responsible for the UX of a product, or a collection of systems. This means prioritizing UX work as necessary and coordinating with junior UX team members to get to the tactical work done. The primary technical differentiators for this role are the abilities to conduct advanced statistical analysis and build reliable surveys. A Ph.D. in Cognitive Psychology provides the background needed for this role, as does a Master's in Statistics (or something similar) plus several years at the UX researcher level.

Principal UX researcher

The responsibilities expand further for the principal UX researcher, who is usually responsible for a line of business and therefore multiple products. As such, this role is also in a team leader position, influencing hiring decisions and determining which products need their own senior UX. This is often a strategic role and may not be a good fit for your senior UX researchers who really are at their best running a usability lab or analyzing mountains of data. Of course this is just an example and you may be able to share the role to balance tactical and strategic aspects - just make sure you understand your people.

Advanced Deliverables

Once your team is starting to hum along, utilizing great research to produce great designs, it's time to spread the word. What I'm calling "Advanced Deliverables" are the syntheses of findings, the "big picture," etc. You can use these to showcase your UX efforts to other departments. A very common and useful way of doing this is with presentations to other teams. Too often UX work is done in isolation, and its output is rolled into a larger release and essentially buried. Building a presentation to highlight UX success stories helps shine some light on the processes and gives your UXers some visibility. Some examples of larger presentations to put together include:

• A portfolio showcasing the evolution of prototypes built by your designers
• The key findings from UX Research across all studies involved in a project (usability testing, heuristic evaluations, contextual in-

quiries, etc.)
• The end-to-end process for a usability survey including recruitment, survey construction, administration, analysis, and reporting
• A "day in the life" demonstration of how different personas go through their work days and use their systems

If you're ready to get even more advanced, you may consider having your UX team collaborate with your Training department on a "User Experience 101" style course. The idea here is to provide an overview of the field, its methods, and its value in order to promote better integration of UX into the company culture. Helpful topics to include are:
• Definitions of user experience, usability engineering, user-centered design, and human-computer interaction
• The discipline of user experience and what it covers
• How UX helps balance user needs with those of business and technology
• Methodology
• Output from UX efforts
• Value of UX efforts
• Incorporating UX into new areas

Why is all this education important?
Without education, people inexperienced with the UX world will misunderstand and misapply what you're working so hard to generate.

From the This Really Happened Files:
One of our "Product Owners" was putting together material for a Business Analyst Summit, kind of an internal conference for BAs. She brought in me along with a UX designer to put together a large schematic of how business analysts thought the UX and BA relationship worked in terms of gathering requirements, handing off requirements for design and then testing, etc. In good UX Research fashion I conducted several interviews with BAs in different departments to get a sense of how they thought the

work flowed between the different job roles. The end result was a large flowchart with swim lanes indicating the different roles and which decisions and tasks belonged to each role. As it was the output of a research project, it was full of misunderstandings, such as a UX researcher conducting a post-deployment usability survey at the beginning of a project (which is impossible). We didn't think much of it since we were just asked to document how the process was *perceived* by the business analysts. So, after weeks of research and building up the flowchart, this report was presented at the BA Summit by the Product Owner (whose own background was business analysis) for all to see. The problem was, she very clearly indicated to the whole room that this was the current state of the *actual* user experience process, not just how it was perceived. That is, we had gone and documented our process with mistakes everywhere, such as that nonsensical surveying of a nonexistent system. Naturally, we were upset. We had done what she had asked, and then she had gone and represented us as a bunch of people who don't understand our own processes and really just didn't know what we were doing. She had not quite understood what she had asked for, and then upon receipt really didn't understand what had been delivered - but that didn't stop her from misrepresenting the expertise and value of our entire department.

/End of File

It's not enough if your UX people know what they're doing. It helps, but it's also not enough when *you* begin to understand what your UX people are doing. *Everyone* needs to understand what is going on with UX, or crazy examples like the one above will happen. To avoid this you need to take your org's maturity up several levels, beyond the basics.

CHAPTER 7: INTERVIEW GUIDE

Interviewing UX people is best conducted in concert with other, experienced UX people. If you don't have any working for you yet, the following guide will be a valuable supplement to the typical interview questions you would ask other prospective employees. It's organized into questions, things you want to hear, and things you don't want to hear. It's not meant to be a black-and-white, or correct/incorrect scoring sheet, but more of a way to feel out if the candidate knows what he or she is talking about.

The General section is about giving the candidates an opportunity to show what UX means to them and provide some background about how they got into the field.

There's a dedicated Data Analysis section for UX researcher candidates. The reason for this is because UX designers are going to have time set aside to show their work in the form of a portfolio or UI demo, while UX researchers are unlikely to have a comparable presentation highlighting their proficiency.

General

1. What does user experience mean to you?
What you're looking for:
• User experience means the end-to-end interaction with a system. Becoming aware of it, using it, getting help or training on it, and replacing it.
• User experience is like usability but is more comprehensive.
• User experience is what people think and feel about a system.

- User experience is "a person's perceptions and responses that result from the use or anticipated use of a product, system or service" (*Note:* The is the ISO definition of UX. Hearing it verbatim in an interview would be pretty impressive.)

What you're *not* looking for:
- User experience is whatever the user tells us. *What's wrong with this?* It's just a lame answer. Anyone who says something like this not only doesn't have experience with the field, they haven't even really thought about it that much.
- User experiences are things we build. *What's wrong with this?* Experience is in the mind of the user. We can design systems, and screens, and products, but we can't really build an experience. We build the things that initiate and support an experience. By the way, a user interface is not an experience.

2. How does user experience differ from usability engineering?
What you're looking for:
- User experience is more holistic, as a discipline.
- User experience is more about the mindset of the user, not the system.
- Usability engineering is a set of methods that are part of the discipline of user experience.

What you're *not* looking for:
- Usability engineering is just the testing methodology that user experience uses. *What's wrong with this?* This conflates usability engineering (a set of methods) with usability testing, which is just one part of usability engineering.
- User experience is about the emotions users feel, how much the system delights them, etc. *What's wrong with this?* User experience can include these things, but that limited view doesn't comprise the whole of user experience.

3. How did you get interested in the field of user experience?
What you're looking for:
- This is an open-ended opportunity for them to show passion

for the field, an interesting anecdote about a personal encounter with a bad user interface, etc. There's no real right or wrong answer, but there are answers that should give you pause.

What you're *not* looking for:
• "I hear it pays well." *What's wrong with this?* Sure, financial compensation is a driver for employment, but this kind of answer speaks to both inexperience and a lazy attitude.
• "I just kind of drifted into it." *What's wrong with this?* Someone who just drifts into a field was probably put there by a manager trying to plug a hole, like making a accountant into an ethnographer. This isn't the kind of work experience that is going to help your org, especially if it's new.

4. Please describe a situation where your work solved a UX issue.
What you're looking for:
• This should be a complete answer with a description of a problem, perhaps even discovery of the problem (like a usability issue or a screen design flaw). From there the candidate should describe how they helped prioritize the issue, get it in front of stakeholders, and advocate for its resolution.

What you're *not* looking for:
• For a researcher: simply making a recommendation about a usability issue. Researchers make recommendations all the time, but not all of them get resolved. You need to hear about how they compared it to other issues, worked with project management and development, and saw the issue changed in a revised version of the system. Bonus points for a follow-up study where it was shown that the issue was fixed (user feedback, fewer IT trouble tickets, etc.).
• For a designer: simply changing something on a screen. You need to hear about how the UI issue was causing a problem, or would cause a problem if implemented. From there empirical evidence about the resolution would help, such as a change in incorrect usage being found in the back end monitoring software.

Data and Analysis (for UX researchers)
1. Please describe qualitative and quantitative data.
What you're looking for:
• Quantitative data means numbers. Things like error rates, time on task, Likert scale values, task completion rates, percent satisfied.
• Qualitative data means words. Things like likes, dislikes, comments, interview summaries.

What you're *not* looking for:
• Quantitative means a high sample size, or "statistically significant." *What's wrong with this?* Quantitative does not mean "more," even though it sounds really similar to "quantity." Statistical significance requires quantitative data, but the two are not interchangeable terms.
• Qualitative data means high quality. *What's wrong with this?* This is someone trying to BS their way through the interview by guessing (incorrectly) that "qualitative" must have something to do with "quality."

2. Please describe subjective and objective data.
What you're looking for:
• Subjective means it's from the mind of the user, like an opinion, a preference, or an interpretation. What they like, what they dislike, how they would improve things, why they made a mistake during a test.
• Objective means it's from outside the mind of the user. Examples include number of errors made during a test, how long it takes to complete a task, and number of users failing a task.

What you're *not* looking for:
• Subjective means qualitative, hard to measure, or vague. *What's wrong with this?* Subjective data can be quantitative, such as a survey item like "I like the new system better than the old system"

with a 1-7 agreement rating scale.
• Objective means quantitative, solid, concrete. *What's wrong with this?* Objective data can be qualitative, such as "I have used this system before." This is qualitative in that it is non-numeric.

3. What are the different levels of measurement in data analysis?
What you're looking for:
• Nominal, which is essentially categorical e.g., "Male" vs. "Female" or "Younger" vs. "Older"
• Ordinal, which is numeric but only the order matters. In a footrace the first place winner crosses the line first, and the second place next. It doesn't matter by how much second place trailed first place. In UX ordinal data might come from ranking features in a system.
• Interval. This is numeric where each value is equidistant from the other. The classic example is a thermometer, where 10 degrees is as far from 20 degrees as it is from zero degrees. However, 20 degrees is not twice as warm as 10 degrees since the zero on the scale is not a true zero. In UX a Likert-type scale with every level assigned a number e.g., [1 2 3 4 5 6 7] can be treated as an interval scale.
• Ratio. Very similar to interval, but with a true zero. In UX this could be a time on task measure, as zero on the scale really means zero time and 60 seconds on a task is really twice as long as 30 seconds.

What you're *not* looking for:
• "High level measurement" and "low level measurement." *What's wrong with this?* These answers don't really mean anything.
• Any combination of objective, subjective, quantitative, qualitative. *What's wrong with this?* These are "close but no cigar" answers. The candidate probably knows just enough about data to be dangerous.

4. What are some parametric statistical techniques in which you're proficient?
What you're looking for:

• T-test, Analysis of Variance (ANOVA, MANOVA, ANCOVA), linear/multiple regression
• Advanced techniques like Factor Analysis are nice to have, but are rarely needed in the UX world.

What you're not looking for:
• "What does parametric mean?" *What's wrong with this?* It's OK for a designer to not know this stuff, but a researcher should. Parametric tests are those that are appropriate for the Interval and Ratio levels of measurement discussed above.
• Any of the nonparametric tests below in Question 5.

5. How about some nonparametric techniques?
What you're looking for:
• Chi Square, Mann-Whitney, Kruskal Wallis, Fisher's Exact Test, Friedman, Sign test, Wald test, logistic regression

What you're *not* looking for:
• "What does nonparametric mean?" *What's wrong with this?* See above re: designers vs. researchers. Nonparametric tests are meant for the Nominal and Ordinal levels of measurement.
• Any of the parametric tests in Question 4.

Methods questions for UX researchers
1. How would you put together a usability test, from beginning to end?
What you're looking for:
• Stages of the test including planning, recruitment, execution, analysis, and reporting.
• Careful consideration of who the end users are, and coordinating with business analysts or others to identify the right users.
• Consideration of hypotheses and variables (what's being investigated and what's being measured).
• Developing an open-ended usability test script that gives users tasks to achieve rather than a sequence of actions to take.

What you're *not* looking for:
• Grabbing random people in the cafeteria without making sure

they're the right kind of user. *What's wrong with this?* Test participants are a sample and should match the population of actual end users; they can't be purely random.

• Anything to do with User Acceptance Testing (rigid scripts, testing for bugs, testing for satisfying business requirements). *What's wrong with this?* UAT is about business requirements and seeing if the system works, not if people are able to figure out the system.

2. What are the advantages and disadvantages of standardized usability scales like the SUS?

What you're looking for:

• Advantage: Can compare scores across applications.

• Advantage: Can compare score of an application with a previous version of the same application's score, for trending over time.

• Advantage: Cost effective. Standardized scales have all the psychometric considerations built in already and don't need a lot of research time to validate.

• Disadvantage: No flexibility in wording of items.

• Disadvantage: Not diagnostic. They can tell you if a system is usable, but you need to add sections such as "Likes" and "Dislikes" to start to understand what the issues are.

What you're *not* looking for:

• "What's a standardized usability scale?" *What's wrong with this?* This person doesn't have enough domain knowledge to run a survey.

• Advantage: Because they're quantitative they can replace usability testing. *What's wrong with this?* Surveys and usability tests have different goals and one doesn't replace the other despite how quantitative they may be.

• Advantage: Standardized just means the scales are the same, like 1 - 5, but you can change the wording to suit your needs. *What's wrong with this?* Standardized means everything is standardized. The scales *and wording* must remain the same.

• Disadvantage: They're proprietary and expensive. *What's wrong with this?* This isn't true - several are completely free like SUS and UMUX.

3. How do you structure a heuristic evaluation? What elements do you report?
What you're looking for:
• A description of the usability issue.
• The heuristic itself that the usability issue violates. There are several sets of these, like Nielsen's and Gerhardt-Powals's.
• How severe the issue is. It could be Showstopper or Severe, or High, Medium, Low, or Cosmetic/Aesthetic.
• A recommendation on how to address the issue. This could be a design change, an interaction fix, or even documenting and training on the issue.

What you're *not* looking for:
• A laundry list of issues with no empirical basis (no heuristics) and no recommendations. *What's wrong with this?* A list of issues is incomplete and non-actionable. The researcher needs to provide heuristics that the issues violate and recommendations.
• No ranking of which issues are most important (severity rating, "Top 5" issues, etc.). *What's wrong with this?* Severity ratings are needed so project managers can prioritize which issues to address.

4. What's the difference between and interview and contextual inquiry?
What you're looking for:
• Contextual inquiry is done in the context of a user's job. It's a mix of observation and interview that takes place where the user works.
• Interviews are more general. They can be done over the phone, or in a conference room. It's less important to see what the user is actually doing. It's easier and cheaper than contextual inquiry, but less informative.

What you're *not* looking for:
• They're basically the same thing. *What's wrong with this?* Contextual inquiry requires the researcher to be onsite observing actual work.
• Contextual inquiry is basically ethnography, and requires the researcher to work with the user for a long time (like days). *What's wrong with this?* Ethnography is longer-term, but contextual inquiry is not always and can be over the course of a couple hours.
• Contextual inquiry is a structured interview about the user's work. It can be done over the phone. *What's wrong with this?* As above, the researcher needs to be with the worker *in the context* of their work.
• Interviews are open-ended and high level. *What's wrong with this?* Interviews can be structured and low level as well.

Methods questions for UX designers

1. What are some different types of prototypes you've helped develop or design?
What you're looking for:
• Low-fidelity prototypes like paper sketches or simple wireframes.
• High-fidelity prototypes like heavily interactive mockups or sandbox systems.

What you're *not* looking for:
• Not knowing what low- and high-fidelity means. *What's wrong with this?* This is basic knowledge for designers.
• Claiming that low-fidelity only means paper prototypes. *What's wrong with this?* Fidelity refers to the realism of the prototype. Clickable wireframes that look like sketches are still low-fidelity.
• Claiming that high fidelity is anything on a computer screen. *What's wrong with this?* As in the above, a static onscreen image is not high-fidelity.

2. In UI design, to what extent should the UI get out of the way of the content on the screen?

What you're looking for:
• Recovery should always be visible. The UI should never disappear with no obvious way to get it back (e.g., with a secret gesture).
• UI design shouldn't follow trends just because they're trends. Flat design doesn't work everywhere. Gray everything doesn't work everywhere.

What you're *not* looking for:
• Content is king. You shouldn't clutter your screen with controls. *What's wrong with this?* If the only person who knows how the thing works, without being taught, is the designer then it's a bad design.
• If Apple and Google are doing it (flat design, gray icons), it must be OK. *What's wrong with this?* Apple and Google get some things wrong. You can't just trust that everything they do will be good for your users.

3. How do you balance the needs of casual and expert users in your UI designs?
What you're looking for:
• Plenty of research to understand the needs and work habits of casuals vs. experts.
• Provide guided processes (like a wizard UI) to walk casual users through complex tasks.
• Retaining a straightforward UI for experts to use once they've mastered the process.
• Provide on-screen help that is readily available but not intrusive to tasks.

What you're *not* looking for:
• Training the users to become experts before they have to use the UI. *What's wrong with this?* Even if this did work (it really doesn't), it's very expensive and time consuming.
• Forcing everyone to use a handholding version of the UI that helps casuals but slows experts down. *What's wrong with this?* You don't want to annoy your most efficient, productive users with an

Kraig Finstad

"easy" interface that slows them down.

CHAPTER 8: CONCLUSION

So, not so common sense after all, is it? The only easy thing about user experience is that it's easy to get wrong. That's why it happens so much. The best defense against getting it wrong is information, and now you should have enough information to start implementing user experience at your company, or within your project, more effectively. At a couple points in this book I've made reference to some UX people having just enough knowledge to be dangerous. I've imparted about that same level of knowledge to you, but I'm trusting that it won't be dangerous in your hands because you are not going to be doing the actual UX work and then providing end users with solutions that don't really meet their needs. You'll be using this knowledge to recognize and reward good work while rejecting the shoddy stuff. You'll be hiring and placing the right people in the right positions based on their expertise, rather than filling slots with people who are the wrong fit. Ultimately, you'll be combining this knowledge with your own expertise to get your company to take UX seriously and improve the bottom line. In fact, you may be in the perfect position to ensure success. Back in the dot-com bubble days, the demand for programmers outstripped supply, and then suddenly everyone became a programmer. Got a little experience making web pages? Hey, you're a programmer! Quantity increased, quality decreased. The thing is, many of those newly minted programmers probably weren't even fully aware of how limited their skillsets were. Today, it's a similar situation with UX. The researcher who turns in a "usability test report" that is really just an issues summary may not know he's doing it wrong. Upper level management is unlikely to know either by reading the executive summary. You will be at the vanguard for higher quality UX work. If low quality UX work becomes pervasive, upper management is going to call it failure of the discipline. You don't want to run into this: "We tried UX and it failed. What else you got?"

An essential point I hope you take away from all of this focus on deliverables is that the basics of user experience are still important. The field (in general) likes to act like usability is a solved problem; it is not. We are not at the point where we can move completely on to emotional experiences and purely aesthetic design choices because everything is already either easy to use or we can just trust that design decisions made by large corporations will work for us. At the beginning of this book I used a phone + map app example to demonstrate how basic human factors issues persist. Throughout the book I've used real-world examples to illustrate how the wrong corporate mindset and inadequate UX efforts have contributed to system designs that are still hard to use. Usability and UX need to be built into the culture of companies from the ground up, and as a manager you have the ability and influence to make that happen. UX needs to be done right, done consistently, and done by the right people for the job.

REFERENCES

Balsamiq Mockups 3 [Computer Software]. (2016). Retrieved from https://www.balsamiq.com

Bangor, A., Kortum, P.T. & Miller, J.T. (2008) An empirical evaluation of the System Usability Scale. International Journal of Human-Computer Interaction, 24, 574–594.

Brooke, J. (1996). SUS: A "quick and dirty" usability scale. In: Jordan, P.W., Thomas, B., 485.

CogTool [Computer Software]. (2015). Retrieved from http://cogtool.hcii.cs.cmu.edu/

Card, Moran, & Newell. (1983). The psychology of human computer interaction. Hillsdale, NJ. Erlbaum Associates.

Finstad, K. (2006). The System Usability Scale and non-native English speakers. Journal of Usability Studies 1 (4), 185–188.

Finstad, K. (2010a). Response interpolation and scale sensitivity: Evidence against 5-point scales. Journal of Usability Studies, 5, 104–110.

Finstad, K. (2010b). The usability metric for user experience. Interacting With Computers, 22, 323–327.

Hackos, J. T. & Redish, J. C. (1998). User and task analysis for interface design. New York, NY. John Wiley & Sons, Inc.

ISO 9241-11 (1998). Ergonomic Requirements for Office Work with Visual Display Terminals (VDTs). Part 11: Guidance on Usability.

Nielsen, J. (1993). Usability Engineering. San Francisco: Morgan Kaufmann.

ABOUT THE AUTHOR

Kraig Finstad spent years in the trenches of user experience after earning his PhD in cognitive psychology. During this time he focused on quantitative methods and usability scale research, such as the creation of the Usability Metric for User Experience. He now works as a consulting statistician in Florida.

www.ingramcontent.com/pod-product-compliance
Lightning Source LLC
Chambersburg PA
CBHW022116170526
45157CB00004B/1671